Dante

Past Masters

George Holmes

DANTE

Oxford Toronto Melbourne
OXFORD UNIVERSITY PRESS
1980

Oxford University Press, Walton Street, Oxford OX2 6DP

OXFORD LONDON GLASGOW
NEW YORK TORONTO MELBOURNE WELLINGTON
KUALA LUMPUR SINGAPORE JAKARTA HONG KONG TOKYO
DELHI BOMBAY CALCUTTA MADRAS KARACHI
NAIROBI DAR ES SALAAM CAPE TOWN

British Library Cataloguing in Publication Data

Holmes, George, b. *1927*
Dante – (Past Masters)
1. Dante Alighieri – Criticism and interpretation
I. Series
851′.1   PQ4390   79–41291
ISBN 0–19–287505–1
ISBN 0–19–287504–3 Pbk

*Printed in Great Britain by
Cox & Wyman Ltd, Reading*

Contents

Acknowledgements

I am indebted to Professor Cecil Grayson and
Mr Charles Parkin for invaluable comments on
earlier drafts of this book.

Translations of the lyric poems are taken
from *Dante's Lyric Poetry*, ed. K. Foster and
P. Boyde (Oxford: Oxford University Press,
1967); of the letters from *Dantis Alagherii
Epistolae*, ed. P. Toynbee, 2nd ed. (Oxford:
Oxford University Press, 1966). Passages
from the Italian text of the *Comedy* are taken
from the *Edizione Nazionale* of the *Società
Dantesca Italiana, Dante Alighieri La Commedia
secondo l'antica vulgata*, ed. Giorgio Petrocchi
(Milan: Arnoldo Mondadori, 1966–7).

List of abbreviations

The following abbreviations have been used
in the text:

Comedy	*Divina Commedia*, Divine Comedy
Conv	*Convivio*, The Banquet
DVE	*De Vulgari Eloquentia*, On Vernacular Expression
Inf	*Inferno*, Hell
Mon	*Monarchia*, Monarchy
Para	*Paradiso*, Paradise
Purg	*Purgatorio*, Purgatory
VN	*La Vita Nuova*, The New Life

Introduction

Dante's *Divine Comedy*, the account of his journey through hell, purgatory and heaven, is one of the world's great poems. It is read chiefly as an achievement of the poetic imagination; but Dante was not only a poet, he was also a philosophical thinker, an active politician, and a religious visionary. To understand the meaning which he intended to convey in his poem and the force which drove him to write, it is necessary to understand the ideas behind it. Dante belongs to the class of men who try to present a general solution to the main intellectual and social dilemmas of their day. Many writers have attempted this, but Dante's success in embodying his answer in poetry is perhaps unsurpassed.

The obvious reason for examining Dante's problems and his solutions to them is to increase our understanding of his poem. But there is another reason too. The problems which Dante confronted and which loom large in his poetry were central. They included, for instance, the relation between human reason and the teaching of the Bible, the relation between sexual love and spiritual love, the conflict between the authority of the Church and the authority of the State, God's influence on the movements of the stars and on human actions. In the form in which Dante faced them, these problems have been made largely obsolete by changes in institutions or by the development of science. But they involve dilemmas which have a permanent interest. In the particular formulations which we find in Dante, they also provide a cross-section of the great issues of European civilisation at the height of the Middle Ages. Dante's *Comedy* (the adjective *Divine* was added after his death) has rightly been regarded as the supreme literary expression of a crucial stage in European thought.

Dante's ideas evolved in response to important experiences. These included both events in his private life, principally the death of Beatrice, the woman who inspired much of his poetry, and events in his turbulent political life, such as his exile from Florence. His thought was in a constant state of evolution, which is one reason why a biographical approach to it is essential.

Another reason is that Dante was an intensely autobiographical writer: in his two most famous works, *Vita Nuova* and the *Comedy*, he is himself the chief character.

Before plunging into his life we must try to imagine the outlines of the intellectual scene in which it was played out. Dante was thirty-five in 1300, the date at which he placed the action of the *Comedy*. Up to that point, the whole of his life had probably been spent in Florence, a booming industrial and commercial city, a wealthy community without much high culture. Part of the Florentine contribution to Dante's mind is simply this city atmosphere, the strong sense of individual personality and individual destiny which city life encourages, and which appears strongly in the *Comedy*. There was also a well-established school of poets in Florence and neighbouring cities, among whom Dante quickly became outstanding. Another important local influence was the profusion of intense religious movements in central Italy, which had no real parallel in Northern Europe.

But the intellectual world which Dante confronted was, for the most part, not Florentine. It was European, and its capital was Paris. It had been framed principally by the development of philosophy and theology at the European universities. The subject with the greatest prestige in the thirteenth-century world was theology – the study of the Bible with the help of Christian commentators. In that field the Bible was the word of God and the ultimate authority. In the faculties of arts, however, in the study of logic and what we would call 'philosophy' and 'science', the ultimate authority was the Greek pagan philosopher Aristotle, who did not appear to believe in the immortality of the soul or the divine creation of the world. The European mind in Dante's day was, to a large extent, dominated by the problem of working out the implications of these two conflicting authorities and trying to reconcile them. The best-known attempt at reconciliation was contained in the works of St. Thomas Aquinas, who died in 1274, when Dante was nine years old.

The conflict of books was in a sense a reflection of the conflict of powers. In the thirteenth century the Church was at the height of its influence as a terrestrial authority, and the papacy was a political force to be reckoned with. It was a common assumption of thinking men that the pope, rather than the king, was the ultimate authority in earthly life. In practice there was constant friction, and this dualism in society created serious dilemmas. Did earthly life have any purpose, apart from the fulfilment of Christian duties and preparation for an immortal afterlife?

Philosophies follow the structure of the societies which frame them. The thirteenth-century Church and State were both strongly monarchical, so the instinct to imagine that all the forces of mind and matter were presided over by a supreme God was strong. But the same society was divided vertically, so that it was obsessed by the conflict between spirit and matter, between religious and rational precepts and explanations. Dante, as we shall see, approached these issues indirectly: as the subject of a city state, not a monarchy; as a well-read layman, not a professional philosopher; and through the problems raised by writing poetry. He eventually found himself facing a number of central, contemporary intellectual questions. He expressed them, as artists do, with an imaginative power which is different from the insight of the professional thinker.

1 The invention of Beatrice

Dante Alighieri was born into an old Florentine family in 1265. He was married, probably about 1283, to Gemma Donati, who is unmentioned in his writings but bore him two sons, both of whom wrote commentaries on his great poem. Though there is no real evidence about the first thirty years of his life, the milieu in which he grew up is well documented: Dante belonged to the class of propertied gentlemen citizens, the natural leaders of an independent city republic. There is a legend that as a young man he fought in a Florentine expedition against the nearby city of Arezzo, and the first reliable biographical facts about him relate to his entry into active political life in 1295. Though not a great centre of learning, Florence was a highly literate society. Some members of Dante's class took a dilettante interest in literature and philosophy, and he must have been included in their number from an early age. It is possible that he even attended the nearest university at Bologna. It is more likely, however, that his culture was derived mainly from Florentine sources: from local teachers of rhetoric, who introduced him to Latin literature, and from the convent schools, where he learned about philosophy and theology. Dante's external life story is sharply divided into two halves by his exile in 1302: thereafter he was a wanderer until his death in 1321. Until 1302 he was probably in many respects a typical Florentine.

But in other respects he was already very untypical. By 1295 he was a famous poet, at least among the connoisseurs of the art in the Tuscan cities. About seventy of his poems survive from those first thirty years of his life. During that period he also composed the extraordinary book called *La Vita Nuova* (The New Life), which was constructed by taking thirty-one of the poems and embedding them in a prose narrative which tells the story of his relationship with a lady called Beatrice, in such a way that the poems are presented as if they had been inspired by stages in that love story. The *VN* and the poems are the only record we have of Dante's life and ideas in this period, and are the subject of this chapter. From the poems in *VN* and others independently preserved, it is clear that Dante started his poetic career by writing in the established tradition of 'courtly love': poems about the torments of unsatisfied love inspired by an unattainable lady. This stage was superseded by a new subject-matter, the celebration of a lady, Beatrice, whose beauty was a reflection of divine goodness. To love her was an enhancement of life, not a torture. The prose part of *VN*, a highly original work, was composed to express this new attitude to life and poetry.

Who was Beatrice? She was born a Portinari and married a Bardi (both richer and more prominent families than Dante's) and she died at the age of twenty-four in 1290. Apart from that, all we know about her is what Dante himself tells us in *VN*, which may be largely imaginary. He first saw her and fell in love with her when he was nine years old, but by the age of eighteen love took hold of him even more completely. He passed through various stages before her early death – concealing his love by writing poems to other ladies, suffering torments of anguish in Beatrice's presence, turning to the composition of poems of pure adoration. The real Beatrice is a shadowy figure. The Beatrice presented in *VN* is a person of overwhelming attractiveness and power. Her personality embodied a quite new conception of feminine goodness, a new image, different from both the idol of erotic verse and the saint of hagiography, but drawing inspiration from both. She is an invention, but an archetypal one, appealing to the deepest emotions, which was not only to be the focus of Dante's own religious idealism but was also, in a less calculable way, to affect ideas of the relationship between art, religion, saintliness and womanhood permanently. Though made so early in his career she is in a sense Dante's most original and profound creation.

The death of Beatrice and the composition of *VN* were succeeded by a period in which Dante composed philosophical poetry of a different kind. Then, probably during the period of philosophical poetry in 1295, came the beginning of his political career, a natural break at which this chapter will end. Political activity in Florence led dramatically to Dante's exile in 1302; in exile he immersed himself in writing philosophical and literary commentaries on his poems, and in politics. Beatrice recedes into the background for more than a decade after *VN*, until she reappears as a central figure of the *Comedy*, the composition of which occupied Dante's later years. She reappears as a redeemed soul in heaven with even greater power than she had had in her former earthly manifestation.

The philosophy of courtly love

The sophisticated poetry written in Dante's Tuscany was a descendant of the courtly love poetry which had been invented in southern France in the twelfth century, the poetry of the troubadours. Courtly love poetry was originally a product of the feudal world of southern France. It celebrated the beauty of a lady and the torments suffered in love by her unsatisfied admirers. True love, inspired by beauty and refinement of manners, was seen by its literary devotees as an ennobling passion, which continued to exalt and torment the lover in spite of the unattainability of the object of his desire.

Dante himself gave the name *Dolce Stil Nuovo* ('sweet new style') (*Purg* XXIV 57) to the variety of the courtly love convention which was developed in Tuscany and practised by the poets of the school with which he was himself associated. The two great masters of the style who preceded Dante, Guido Guinizelli and Guido Cavalcanti, came from prominent families of Bologna and Florence, and like Dante were city dwellers. When Dante first came on to the literary scene, sometime in the 1280s, Cavalcanti, an older man, was the best poet writing in Florence, and Dante for a time submitted to his influence, calling him later 'my first friend'. From this association sprang his concern with poetry as a vehicle for expressing philosophical and religious values, as Guinizelli and Cavalcanti were themselves amateur philosophers. When they emphasised in their poetry the fruitless torments, rather than the ennobling exaltation, of unrequited love, they made use of the terminology of contemporary natural science. The result was that they produced poetry about the passion of love which was in certain respects scientifically pessimistic: a faint parallel might be a twentieth-century poet dissecting his amours with the tools of Freudian psychology.

To understand this poetry, it is necessary to bear in mind some of the principles of physiology which had been inherited from the ancient Greeks and which were accepted as scientific commonplaces by the intelligentsia of the thirteenth century. The human soul in this scheme was divided into three parts: the vegetative, sensitive and rational, operating in the body through three faculties, the natural spirit in the liver, the vital spirit in the heart and the animal spirit in the brain. The animal spirit worked in the brain as imagination, reasoning and memory. The body was kept in motion by 'spirits' moving along the arteries and nerves. The mechanism of love was that the impression made upon the eyes by a beautiful lady sent spirits moving to the heart, the seat of the emotions, from which other spirits informed the reasoning and memory faculties in the brain.

Many of Cavalcanti's poems therefore speak of love entering through the eyes, attacking the heart, driving away its spirits, destroying its strength, so that the pain is unbearable, as the sighs emerging from it show. These conventional expressions, partly derived from earlier poets of courtly love, entered into the stream of love poetry flowing down even to the twentieth century, so that they appear to the modern reader as the stalest of metaphors and personifications. In the thirteenth century they were just as much the expression of a living view of man's nature as ideas of 'repression' or 'neurosis' would be in the twentieth: particularly so in the poets of the *Dolce Stil Nuovo* – including Dante – because of their self-consciously intellectual approach to love. The intellectualisation reached its height in a famous poem called *Donna mi prega* ('A Lady begs me'), in which Guido Cavalcanti set out his theory of the nature of love. Cavalcanti says that love is an 'accident' in the philosophical sense, a separable quality like the whiteness of a sheet of paper, not a separate substance, like the paper itself. It is an obscurity, a blemish on the sensitive soul caused by a vision received by the eyes, and is affected by the conjunction of the stars at the lover's birth. He is particularly anxious to emphasise that it is an irrational force, which does not take effect in the rational part of the soul. It is received in the 'possible intellect', the faculty of understanding, only as an abstract form. It is destructive of virtue in the sense that virtue requires a balance, while love is an excessive force.

Cavalcanti writes *de haut en bas*, an intellectual addressing the ignorant, saying in effect, 'Love is just a powerful emotion for which there is a physical explanation, it doesn't put you in touch with truth or goodness, quite the reverse indeed.' We have to allow for a certain amount of civilised humour in Cavalcanti's poetry, which perhaps should not be taken as completely serious.

The poem touches, however, on a central philosophical issue in late thirteenth-century scholasticism which will reappear in later writings of Dante. The 'possible intellect' is a concept derived from Aristotle's *De Anima* (On the Mind or Soul), the book from which the thirteenth-century university philosophers took much of their psychological theory. Aristotle, the Greek philosopher of the fourth century B.C., was rediscovered in Western Europe in the thirteenth century, and his works were widely used as textbooks. In this book Aristotle emphasised that the intellectual power of rational understanding was separate from the power of emotional feeling. Thirteenth-century users of Aristotle differed about the degree of this separateness. Christian doctrine required, of course, that the human soul should be a single imperishable entity embracing both the emotional and the rational faculties, and this was the interpretation adopted by most orthodox philosophers. One prominent group of interpreters, however, adopting the ideas put forward by the Arabic commentator Averroes, argued that, whatever Christian doctrine might say, Aristotle believed in a real separation: emotional faculties which died with the body, and a separate imperishable intellect. Averroes believed that the possible intellect, the power to comprehend in an individual man, was not an inseparable part of his unique soul but part of a universal intellect, which did not perish with the individual body. 'Averroists' therefore tended towards a materialist interpretation of emotions, coupled with a separate universal power of understanding, implanted temporarily in individual men. No one claimed that this was good Christianity, but many claimed that it was good Aristotelianism, and because of Aristotle's accepted authority in all matters of philosophy and science it was fairly widely taught in the universities, including those of Bologna and Padua from which a Florentine layman might well have picked up such ideas. The problem of the possible intellect troubled Dante and was dealt with explicitly in the *Comedy*. *Donna mi prega* shows dramatically the connection between poetry and live philosophical issues which Dante inherited. We must assume that, under the influence of a teacher like Cavalcanti, poetry and philosophical speculation were connected in Dante's mind from an early stage.

In the period from about 1283, when the first poems were written, to 1295, when he made his first public appearances in city politics, Dante's writing seems to have gone through three main stages. Firstly, there is the period of apprenticeship under *Dolce Stil Nuovo* influences, the strongest of which was Cavalcanti, extending to the early 1290s. Secondly, there is the period of poetry written in praise of Beatrice, culminating in her death in 1293 and the composition of *VN*. Thirdly, there is a period of philosophical poetry.

Dante's early poems are conventional love poetry concerned very largely with the effects – usually intensely painful – of unrequited love. An example of the manner is *Deh, Violetta, che in ombra d'Amore*

> Deh, Violetta, che in ombra d'Amore
> ne gli occhi miei sì subiti apparisti,
> aggi pietà del cor che tu feristi,
> che spera in te e disïando more.
>
> Tu, Violetta, in forma più che umana,
> foco mettesti dentro in la mia mente
> col tuo piacer ch'io vidi;
>   poi con atto di spirito cocente
> creasti speme, che in parte mi sana
> là dove tu mi ridi.

Ah, Violetta, you who so suddenly appeared to my eyes in Love's shadow, pity the heart that puts its trust in you and is dying of desire.

You, Violetta, in a more than human form, You kindled a fire in my mind through the heart, that I saw; and then by the action of a fiery spirit you quickened a hope that partly heals me when you smile at me . . .

Here, drawn from the long tradition of courtly love, are the disturbing power of the vision of beauty, the resulting turbulence of heart and mind, the 'spirits' transmitting effects through the body. A more bizarre example to our eyes is *A ciascun'alma presa e gentil cor* ('To every captive soul and noble heart') – this first line is itself an evocation of much of the contemporary poetic love theory – which became the first poem in *VN*. It describes a dream in which Love appeared holding Dante's heart in one hand and bearing his Lady asleep in his arms. Love awoke the Lady, fed her with the heart and went away weeping.

About 1293 Dante put together the selection of his poems in *VN*, linking them with a prose commentary as episodes in the story of his love for Beatrice. *VN* starts with his first sight of her at the age of nine and goes through the years of torment and adoration to her death. More than a year after her death, we are told, he was consoled by another lady who, for a time, won his affection, but he eventually returned to his devotion to the dead Beatrice and with this reaffirmation the book ends.

VN begins with poems which belong to the early phase of courtly love poetry which has just been described. Dante passes through a stage in which the effect of Beatrice's love on him is so overwhelming that it reduces him to fainting, to illness and almost to death. The poems used in this section were drawn from a stratum of verse in which the Cavalcantian idea of love as a disruptive, almost fatal power was dominant. *Lo doloroso amor che mi conduce a fin di morte* ('The sorrowful love that leads me to final death'), for example, contains the first mention of Beatrice in Dante's works, though it was not used in *VN*. It is a statement that the withdrawal of the light of Beatrice's eyes causes such sorrow that he expects to die. If his soul is then consigned to torment for his sins, its total absorption in love of Beatrice will make it indifferent to the penalty.

Beatrice

The movement to what I have defined as the second phase in Dante's early development – the phase in *VN* of adoration of Beatrice – begins with the poem *Donne ch'avete intelletto d'amore* ('Ladies who have understanding of love'), which Dante himself later singled out as the beginning of his 'new rhymes' (*nove rime*) (*Purg* XXIV 50). Introducing the poem in *VN*, Dante says he decided to stop bewailing his own condition and console himself instead by writing poems in praise of Beatrice. Whatever its real origin, this is such a poem, and it is in sharp contrast to the morbid analysis of the poet's own emotions which had been his stock-in-trade up to this point. The poetic viewpoint swung round completely from introspection to adoration of a woman, so wonderful on earth that heaven craved her presence:

An angel cries in the divine intellect, saying: 'Lord in the world there appears a marvel in act, proceeding from a soul whose splendour reaches even here on high!' Heaven, whose only lack is the lack of her, begs her from its Lord, and every saint cries out for this favour.

While she remains on earth she is not only exquisitely beautiful but also a fountain of grace ennobling everyone she touches:

When she finds someone worthy to see her, he receives the full effect of her power; for what she then gives him turns to his good and happiness, and renders him so humble that he forgets every injury. Again, God has given her this greater grace, that no one who has spoken with her can come to an evil end.

When he celebrates Beatrice's death, the poet's anguish is not the self-regarding sorrow of the unsuccessful lover but the grief of the mourner. The last poem of the *VN* is *Oltra la spera che più larga gira*:

> Oltre la spera che più larga gira
> passa 'l sospiro ch'esce del mio core:
> intelligenza nova, che l'Amore
> piangendo mette in lui, pur su lo tira.
>
> Quand'elli è giunto là dove disira,
> vede una donna, che riceve onore,
> e luce sì, che per lo suo splendore
> lo peregrino spirito la mira.

Beyond the sphere that circles widest passes the sigh that issues from my heart: a new understanding which Love, lamenting, imparts to him, draws him ever upwards. When he arrives where he desires to be, he sees a Lady who receives honour and who shines so that the pilgrim spirit contemplates her for her splendour.

'The sphere that circles widest' is the outermost circle of the heavens rotating, according to medieval cosmology, around the earth. Beyond that lies Heaven itself. Love, now quite different in its effects from the conventional type of courtly love, gives the spirit, issuing from the lover, the power to rise into Heaven and see Beatrice already enthroned there.

We know nothing about Beatrice's character which would help to explain the poetic and intellectual revolution in Dante's mind which is associated with her name. How, then, was this transformation of attitude inspired? One prominent strand in *VN* is a debate with Cavalcanti and with the Cavalcantian theory of love. When Dante describes his encounter with Beatrice at the age of nine he uses the usual physiological terminology: the animal spirit dwelling with the sensitive spirits in the brain speaks to the

spirit of sight, the natural spirit in the stomach becomes appre-
hensive. But he takes care in the prose commentary to emphasise
that this was a love in which reason had a part too: 'her image
was of such very noble virtue that it did not suffer Love to rule
me without the faithful counsel of reason'. Much later on (cap
25), after expounding a poem in which 'Love' appears as a personification, he explains elaborately that this is not due to philosophical naïvety, but is a conscious rhetorical device. After
explaining that he personifies Love in the same way as Ovid did,
he ends

it would be shameful if anyone put things into verse in figurative form
or rhetorically and, when asked, could not separate his words from
that clothing so that they should be truly understood. And I and my
first friend [Cavalcanti] are well aware of people who write poetry in
that silly way.

Towards the end of *VN*, *Gentil pensero che parla di vui* ('A
gentle thought that speaks of you'), addressed to the new Lady
who temporarily supplanted the dead Beatrice, says that a new
love has entered the heart which the heart has to explain to the
soul. Dante explains in the prose exposition 'that it seems proper
to call the appetite "heart" and the reason "soul" will be obvious
to those to whom I wish it to be clear'. These passages show that
the audience for which Dante intended *VN* was an audience of
learned poets familiar with the philosophical and rhetorical implications of his language, and also suggest that he was dis-
tinguishing himself from those who thought that reason was not
concerned with love. He was proclaiming his understanding of
the language of Cavalcantian physiological pessimism, but also
dissociating himself from some of its implications.

   The relationship with Cavalcanti appears more graphically at
one point. Before the death of Beatrice in *VN* Dante incorporates
a poem, *Io mi senti' svegliar* ('I felt a sleeping spirit of love
awaken'), in which he sees the Lady of Cavalcanti's poems, Giovanna, approaching him with his own Lady, Beatrice. Love says
to him: 'This one is Spring, and the other's name is Love, so
much does she resemble me.' When he attached it to the prose of
VN, Dante gave this poem a much more dramatic significance.
In the prose exposition preceding the poem, he now reported
these words, said to him by Love:

That first lady is called Spring (*Primavera*) only because of her coming today, for I inspired the one who gave her the name to call her spring, that is she shall come first (*prima verrà*) on the day that Beatrice shall show herself according to the imagination of him who is faithful to her. And if you will consider her original name, that too says 'she shall come first' because her name Giovanna comes from that John who preceded the true light, saying 'I am the voice of one crying in the wilderness; prepare ye the way of the Lord.'

The assimilation of Cavalcanti's Lady to John the Baptist and Dante's to Jesus Christ is an extraordinary apotheosis of the Lady of courtly love poetry.

Dante's own works give us very little help in explaining Beatrice. The general influence of religious and philosophical reading may have encouraged a conversion which made Dante an idealist, but it does not explain the specific creation of the figure of Beatrice as she appears in *VN*. To explain the invention of Beatrice we have to look not to intellectual influences but to religious example. Beatrice is presented as a woman of supreme beauty, virtue and power; both an object of love and a saint. Dante belonged to a sophisticated city intelligentsia, some of whom were sceptics, but any attempt to reconstruct his environment must also take account of the fact that central Italy in the thirteenth century was exceptionally rich in popular religious movements. Much of this enthusiasm was connected with the religious orders, especially the Franciscans, founded by St Francis at the beginning of the century. It would have been as impossible for a thinking Florentine to avoid being powerfully impressed by these movements as it would for a Victorian to be unconscious of nonconformity, and we must imagine them as a constant part of Dante's background. The Franciscans and Dominicans, who were at this time building the largest churches in Florence, were the most prominent organisations in a flood of movements, both ecclesiastical and lay, which made Tuscany and Umbria in the thirteenth century unusually rich in religious experience and expression. The feature of this religious life which is relevant to the figure of Beatrice is the holy woman. She was a common type in the towns and villages of central Italy. Dante would certainly have known of such women; not only, for example, St. Clare, the founder of the Franciscan women's order, but also less famous women such as his contemporary, St. Margaret of Cortona. The written lives of these saints tell us of conversion, devotion to the apostolic life, miracles, influences over people around them, wish for death. It was probably the impression made on Dante's mind by the female saint, living as a 'mirror of Christ', which turned the Lady of courtly love into Beatrice. Beatrice is the product of a leap of the imagination which joined the erotic beauty of the object of courtly love with the spiritual authority of the saint.

The echoes of hagiography begin in the poems of praise of Beatrice, starting with *Donne ch'avete*. Heaven cries out for her: 'An angel cries in the divine intellect', 'every saint cries out for this favour'. They are intense in Dante's report of his vision of Beatrice's coming death in *Donna Pietosa* ('A compassionate lady'):

I raised my eyes, wet with tears, and saw the angels like a shower of manna returning on high to heaven; and a small cloud went before them, and following it they all cried, 'Hosannah!'.

In the prose of the *VN* Beatrice is from the first invested with the powers of the saint, disseminating grace and humility about her. The poems of praise are addressed to her devotees.

This most noble lady was held in such grace by the people that when she went along the street people ran to see her . . . And when she was near to someone, such humility came into his heart that he dared not raise his eyes, and of this many who experienced it could be my witness to anyone who did not believe it. She went about crowned and clothed with humility, showing no pride in what she saw and heard. Many said when she had passed: 'This is not a woman but one of the most beautiful angels of heaven.'

The stages in her life and in Dante's relations with her are connected with the ideal number nine: Dante is nine when he sees her first, he sees her again nine years later, she died – according to a tortuous calculation involving different calendars – in the ninth day of the ninth month of the ninetieth year, 'to show that she was a nine, that is a miracle whose root is solely in the marvellous Trinity' (*VN* XXIX 3). At her death the 'lord of justice' called her 'to live in glory, under the banner of that blessed queen the virgin Mary, whose name was spoken with the greatest reverence by this blessed Beatrice'.

Dante's encounter with her is presented as a conversion; in

fact his conversion rather than the story of Beatrice is the subject of the book. It begins 'In that part of the book of my memory before which there is little that one can read, is a rubric which says: The New Life begins' (*VN* I 1). The 'book of memory', in the sense of the interior record, and the 'new life' are phrases which carried traditional Christian connotations of a spiritual journey and conversion. Although he incorporated earlier poetry into the fictional story, Dante appears to have been recording a change of outlook and belief which now separated him from his old poetic allegiance to Cavalcanti. He had come to regard love as a redeeming religious force, not the destructive emotion of courtly love poetry. Whether or not Cavalcanti took seriously the philosophical materialism implied in Averroes' interpretation of Aristotle as it appears in his poetry, Dante certainly did. Eventually it repelled him, and in *VN* he recorded a conversion to idealism, which is at the root of all his later ideas.

Dante would have been a major innovator in Italian literature even if he had written nothing to follow *VN*. The poetry which he had written was more graceful and flexible than that of his predecessors, and he had applied his poetic skill to the expression of a new kind of ideal love. In the prose of *VN* he had theorised about the modes of expression and the subject-matter of love poetry. Italian poetry was then a relatively young art, and *VN* represented a great step forward in literary self-consciousness. The achievements for which Dante is chiefly to be remembered were, of course, to come in his future writings. The expansion of his interests into philosophy and politics, without which the argument of the *Comedy* would be unthinkable, was almost entirely part of his future thought. But he had already created Beatrice, the heroine of the *Comedy*, and declared for the first time the religious idealism with which the *Comedy* was to be infused.

The Lady Philosophy

After *VN*, in the mid-1290s, Dante composed a group of poems of a new kind: poems intended to convey philosophical ideas. A decade later, and in very different circumstances, about 1304–8, he composed the book called *Convivio* (The Banquet) which contains commentaries on some of the philosophical poems. *Conv* also contains ideas which arose out of the period in which it was written and are rather tenuously connected with the poetry of *circa* 1294–6, so it will be considered independently in the next chapter. It gives us, however, one piece of information which is essential for our understanding of the philosophical poetry and must therefore be introduced at this point.

Some of these philosophical poems are addressed to a lady. Dante explains that she is not, as she might appear to be, a courtly love lady but an allegorical figure, standing for Philosophy. Allegory, the device of using people or events to stand for abstract ideas, such as a debate between characters representing lust and chastity, was very common in medieval literature and will later play a part in the *Comedy*. It requires explanation in this case because some of the philosophical poems would otherwise appear to be simply following the courtly love convention. Dante also feels bound to explain how the allegorical lady came to take the place of Beatrice in his poetry. He says that, some time after Beatrice's death, he turned for consolation to books of philosophy:

I set myself to read that book of Boethius [*The Consolation of Philosophy*], in which he consoled himself for his anxiety and banishment. And then, hearing that Cicero had written another book dealing with *Friendship*, in which he had reported words of consolation of the excellent Laelius at the death of his friend Scipio, I set myself to read that too. And although I had difficulty in understanding them I finally made as much progress as I could with the aid of my knowledge of grammar and a little of my native wit, by which I had already seen many things almost as if in dreaming, as may be read in the *Vita Nuova*. (*Conv* II xii 1)

Eventually he was so captivated by Philosophy that he came to see her as a 'noble lady' and to pursue his new interests by attending the schools maintained by the Franciscans and Dominicans. 'So that in a short time, perhaps thirty months, I began to feel her sweetness so much that that love drove out and destroyed every other thought.' And so he went on to the new philosophical poetry.

These passages create an acute literary problem, because *VN* also records a conflict in Dante's mind after Beatrice's death between attraction to a new lady and devotion to Beatrice's memory. It would be natural to suppose that it is the same conflict. But in *VN* Beatrice eventually triumphs in death over the other lady, who appears to represent only a temporary revival of the erotic courtly love imagery. In *Conv* the new lady is identified as the Lady Philosophy who progressively replaces Beatrice. No theory has successfully resolved this puzzling contradiction. It seems clear, however, that Dante did develop a new passion for philosophy in the years following the death of Beatrice and the composition of *VN*.

What sources of academic learning were available to him? Florence itself was not a great intellectual centre: it had no university and, therefore, no communities of scholars comparable with those of Paris or Padua. University learning was represented chiefly in the Dominican and Franciscan convents whose schools Dante tells us he attended. Among their friars were men who had been to universities and who were capable of introducing him to classical and scholastic philosophy. They were not themselves top-flight thinkers. We can trace no specific contacts between Dante and the religious. The only local thinker to whom Dante expresses a personal debt is a quite different kind of person, the notary Brunetto Latini, who greets him as his 'son' in canto XV of *Inferno* in the *Comedy*. Brunetto was a layman, a moderately important figure in city politics and famous for the composition of the *Trésor*, a compendium of knowledge written in French but widely read in Italian translation, which introduces the reader to many subjects, among others to Aristotelian and Ciceronian ethics, rhetoric and history. It is unoriginal in its contents but novel in its purpose of introducing the untutored layman to learned culture.

The mendicant orders and the class to which Brunetto belonged between them embraced most of the high culture available in Dante's Florence. The nearest university was at Bologna, which Dante may well have visited, but the probability is that up to 1302 his culture was largely Florentine. If it is true, as Dante tells us in *Conv* (IV i 8), that his pursuit of Philosophy was interrupted at one stage during this period by his perplexity about the highly technical question of God's creation of primal matter, he must already have been deeply interested in scholastic issues. But we simply do not know how much of the expertise which he later demonstrated in the philosophical commentaries in *Conv* had been acquired by 1295.

The only direct evidence which we have for Dante's thought at

this period – the mid 1290s – is contained in a handful of remarkable poems. The first of the philosophical allegories is *Voi
che 'ntendendo il terzo ciel movete* ('O you who move the third
heaven by intellection'). It is addressed to the angels in the circle
of Venus, whose movement influences the course of love on earth,
and expresses a tension between old and new interests. Dante has
been distracted from the lady in heaven, Beatrice, by a new lady,
the power of whose eyes would frighten him away, did he not
expect, by devotion to her, to 'see the beauty of such high marvels
...'. By the time he wrote *Amor che ne la mente mi ragiona*
('Love speaking in my mind'), Philosophy, still personified by a
lady, had become clearly established as an agent of transmission,
standing between inaccessible divine truth and weak human
reason. Philosophy is like an angel in the sense that it is a pure
intelligence, capable of absorbing divine truth and passing some
of it on to grosser natures below. Philosophy has literally what
the Lady has allegorically, the power of strengthening human
faith and displaying the joys of Paradise.

The books which, Dante tells us, inspired him at this time were
Cicero's *De Amicitia* (On Friendship) and Boethius' *Consolation of Philosophy*. They were both popular in the Middle
Ages, yet both far removed from the technicalities of thirteenth-
century university philosophy. They were readable books of the
sort that a thoughtful layman, with a good grounding in Latin,
would turn to, not university textbooks. Cicero, the Roman politician and man of letters, was a pagan and his book gives pagan
moral instruction on the value of friendship, inspired by the
death of a friend. Boethius' book, though written by an Italian
Christian in the sixth century A.D., is not specifically Christian.
His attitude is neoplatonic: that is to say that he sees the universe
as consisting of a central divinity, which is the source of goodness, and everything else in it as good, in so far as it participates
in the pure spirit emanating from the divinity. The 'consolation'
which he advocates is an awareness of God, as identified with
goodness and the source of beatitude, and of the negativity of
evil. Boethius put his teaching into the mouth of a 'Lady Philosophy', who was probably the inspiration for Dante's new lady,
a very different figure from Beatrice. It may also have been as a
result of reading Boethius that Dante adopted a vision of the
universe governed by the principles of emanation from a divine

centre of pure light and goodness, which now first appears in his writings. A metaphysic of this kind is what the poems most strongly suggest, for instance in *Amor che movi tua vertù da cielo,* which was not among the poems interpreted in *Conv*:

Love, who send down your power from heaven as the sun does its splendours – for the greater the perfection of what its beams encounter, the more its influence takes effect: and just as it dispels darkness and cold, so do you, mighty Lord, drive baseness from the heart.

The books and the poems suggest that Dante's new inspiration was a general enthusiasm for the spiritual side of life rather than technical Christian scholasticism.

Towards the end of this phase, however, Dante began to write poetry which went beyond an allegorical use of the courtly love convention to undisguised philosophical speculation. The beginning of *Le dolci rime d'Amor* says plainly

> Le dolci rime d'amor ch'i solia
> cercar ne' miei pensieri,
> convien ch'io lasci
>
> . . . .
>
> diporrò giù lo mio soave stile,
> ch'i' ho tenuto nel trattar d'amore;
> e dirò del valore,
> per lo qual veramente omo è gentile,
> con rima aspr'e sottile.

The sweet love-poetry I was accustomed to seek out in my thoughts I must now forsake . . . I will lay down that style of mine which I held to in writing of love, and I will speak instead in harsh and subtle rhymes concerning the quality by which man is truly noble.

And he goes on to set out an argument about the true nature of 'nobility', disputing the view that it is based on riches and noble birth, advocating instead the idea that nobility is the innate virtue of a man, stemming from an inborn characteristic implanted by God at birth. This poem is an argument in which poetry has been taken over by rational discourse. It also shows evidence of the use of a textbook of university philosophy, the Latin translation of Aristotle's *Ethics* with a commentary by the thirteenth-century theologian, St. Thomas Aquinas.

By about 1296 Dante had moved two stages beyond the courtly love poetic convention in which he had started to write. First he had adapted the poetic style to the presentation of a different kind of emotion, the awe inspired by a woman who combined beauty and religious authority. Then he had adapted it again for the exposition of quite abstract ideas. In making these innovations he had transformed poetic usage, and had stretched the capacity of poetry in order to express an idealism which was religious or philosophical in character. He had thus revealed his characteristic gift for fusing an elaborate abstract meaning with poetic elegance, the gift which he was to develop to still undreamt-of heights in the *Comedy*. Before that happened new ranges of experience were to transform his attitudes and interests.

2 Politics, exile and the inspiration of philosophy

City politics

From 1295 to 1302 Dante was actively engaged in Florentine politics, a career which ended suddenly in exile. The events which led up to his exile, though they were dramatic enough at the time, also had a significance for Dante which changed, and in some respects became greater, as the years went by. As he looked back later in life, the central moment in his life was not his exile in 1302, but Easter 1300, the date at which he chose to set his journey through the other world in the *Comedy*. The obsession with turning-points was characteristic of Dante. He saw his life, retrospectively, as passing through phases of thought, redirected by events. For most of his life we have only the information which he himself chose to give us. Easter 1300, however, is the beginning of a short period in which his biography is relatively clearly illuminated by independent documents. We know enough about the external circumstances to see that this time was really, as well as symbolically, the point at which his personal destiny was caught in the stream of conflict between the great spiritual and temporal powers of the world.

In 1295 and 1296 there are records of Dante taking part in meetings of city councils. His political career began in the aftermath of a great political crisis, the conflict between the 'magnates' (great men) and the 'popolo' (the trading and shopkeeper community), which produced a more egalitarian constitution, the Ordinances of Justice, in 1293. This revolutionary period in Florentine history was followed by an uneasy calm. By 1295, the former rulers of Florence, the broad oligarchy of great 'Guelf' families, had recovered control. In the middle of the thirteenth century Florence had been split between Guelf and Ghibelline families. The Guelfs, in Florence and elsewhere, were traditionally supporters of the power of the pope in central Italy, the Ghibellines of the German emperor, who claimed authority in Italy too. By the 1290s Florence had become firmly Guelf and many Ghibellines were still in exile. But soon after the restoration of political stability in 1295, the Guelf party itself began to show signs of splitting into two factions, which were later to become known as the Black and White Guelfs. One faction, more conservative, was led by Corso Donati, an exemplar and protagonist of magnate attitudes; the other by a rich banker, Vieri de'Cerchi.

Dante had connections with leading politicians of the day on both sides. His socially much more eminent friend, the poet Guido Cavalcanti, was a well-known personal enemy of Corso Donati and was remembered for his contemptuously aristocratic demeanour in politics, as in poetry. But surviving incongruously among Dante's early poems there is an exchange of verses between Dante and Corso Donati's brother, Forese, probably written about 1293–5. Unlike the rest of Dante's work these verses are crudely comic, the exchange of insults rising to the point of Dante casting doubt on Forese's parentage. They illustrate Dante's position in a world in which poetry and politics were both fairly widespread activities of a social élite.

But it would scarcely be credible that Dante should have pursued politics – any more than poetry – merely as an occupation for gentlemen, and there is just enough evidence to suggest that from the first his position in politics was an idealistic one. Placed in the context of 1295, its approximate date, one of the great poems of the period of philosophical poetry, *Le dolci rime d'amor* ('The sweet love-poetry'), has a flavour of commentary on the contemporary political scene. The definition of nobility which Dante attacked in that poem, 'long-standing possession of wealth together with pleasing manners', is just such a definition as would have suited the magnate supporters of Corso Donati. Dante's more elaborate philosophical alternative, drawn from some acquaintance with Aristotle's *Ethics* and summed up as 'the seed of happiness placed by God in a well-disposed soul', is, in contrast, deliberately egalitarian. Though derived from an old poetic theme, the fully developed argument in the poem appears to be a comment on the burning political issue of the day.

When Dante reappears in the political records in the summer of 1300, a new political crisis is developing. The conflict between the Cerchi and Donati factions, later to become known as the White and Black Guelfs respectively, had become more intense. Corso Donati had been banished. In exile he had established influence at Rome with Pope Boniface VIII, an aggressive promoter of the interests of the papacy. Corso persuaded Boniface that the present rulers of Florence were unreliable. In this way he opened a rift between the pope and the ruling Whites, which he hoped to use to secure his own restoration. In the spring of 1300 – the decision was taken about Easter – the Florentine leaders decided to prosecute a group of Florentine businessmen at the papal court, allies of Corso, for working against the interests of the commune. Thus, by a process of mounting distrust between the two governments at Florence and Rome, the political divisions within the city were linked with the interests of outside powers. It was in this way that a Florentine citizen, who had taken up a position in the native politics of his city, could as a result find himself caught up in the politics of Europe.

Dante was associated with the Whites. He was very likely a party to the decision to prosecute Florentines at the papal court. For two months in 1300 he was a Prior, that is one of the six men who held supreme office in the commune. As such he had to confirm the city's stand against the Pope's intervention. He was thus deeply involved in city politics, marked out by identification with the ruling faction and already the object of a papal condemnation, directed against the rulers of the city. His political baptism of fire had been swift.

For more than a year after his priorate Dante remained prominent in the city. On 1 November 1301, the brother of the King of France, Charles of Valois, acting as an agent of Boniface, entered Florence with a substantial army. Once inside he allowed the Blacks to carry out a *coup d'état* which completely reversed the political situation and led to the exile or prosecution of the White leaders. When Charles of Valois came Dante was probably away on a mission to Rome, a last-minute attempt to halt the action of the French invaders, and it is likely that he never saw the inside of Florence again after October 1301. On 27 January 1302 he was sentenced, in his absence, to a fine and exile for financial corruption in office and for conspiring against the Pope, Charles of Valois, and the city. On 10 March he was condemned to death, a sentence which could not be carried out because he was already in exile with many of his political associates.

The sentence against him was obviously a political action; there is no reason to suppose that he had really been guilty of corruption. Nor is there any reason to suppose that Dante was hostile to the papacy as such on the grounds of a general hostility to the exercise of temporal power by spiritual authority. This became a major concern later in his life, but it was not yet prominent in his mind. Nevertheless he had been condemned, however unjustly, by the pope and as an enemy of the pope, and the mark of that condemnation remained on him.

The only statement by Dante which we can be fairly sure gave expression to reflections on the exile close to the event, places his political misfortune in a philosophical framework. It is contained in one of his great lyric poems, *Tre Donne* (Three Ladies). This was probably written within the period 1302–4. It is a further adaptation of the imagery of courtly love to the exposition of an abstract theory. The Lord of Love who occupies Dante's heart sees three women outside it, whose striking beauty and dignity are in contrast with their neglected outcast condition. One, wearing a torn dress, announces herself as Justice and indicates that the others are her daughter and granddaughter. Love, aroused by their plight, proclaims, though human virtues have so fallen on evil days, 'let the eyes that weep and the mouths that wail be those of mankind whom it concerns, having fallen under the rays of such a heaven; not ours, who are of the eternal citadel.' Love acknowledges the proper role of Justice. In the later part of the poem Dante refers more directly to his own plight. He takes pride in being an exile, like the exiled personification of Justice, but he ends by sending his poem off in search of reconciliation.

> Canzone, uccella con le bianche penne;
> canzone, caccia con li neri veltri,
> che fuggir mi convenne,
> ma far mi poterian di pace dono.
> Però nol fan che non san quel che sono.

Song, go hawking with the white wings [White Guelfs]; song, go hunting with the black hounds [Black Guelfs] – which I have had to flee, though they could still make me the gift of peace. It is because they don't know what I am that they don't do so.

Tre Donne may have been written at a moment when Dante hoped that reconciliation was possible. But its most striking feature is the appearance of the concept of Justice. His sense of being the victim of injustice gave importance to an abstract concept of Justice, which was to appear in metamorphosed forms in later writings. Here he probably intends the mother, daughter and granddaughter to represent a hierarchy of levels of justice such as Aquinas had proposed: divine justice, human justice and positive law, each consistent with and derived from the level above. By making Love acknowledge the hierarchy of Justice, Dante placed the concept within a metaphysical view of the world.

Exile

Dante was to be an exile for the rest of his life:

Since it was the pleasure of the citizens of the most beautiful and famous daughter of Rome, Florence, to cast me out of her sweet bosom – in which I was nurtured up to the summit of my life and in which, with its good will, I desired with all my heart to rest my tired spirit and end the days allowed to me – I have gone through nearly all the regions to which the [Italian] tongue extends, a wanderer, almost begging, showing against my will the wound of fortune, often unjustly held against him who is wounded. I have been truly a ship without sail or rudder, carried to many ports and straits and shores by the dry wind blown by grievous poverty, and I have appeared to the eyes of many who had perhaps imagined me, through a certain fame, in another way. (*Conv* I iii)

Political exile was a normal expedient in the city state and his fate was not very uncommon. Nevertheless, it dominated his life. Political exile means isolation and dependence on the patronage of sympathisers. For the thinker it often means a craving for recognition, an obsession with self-justification, passionate attachment to the ideas which give meaning to a rootless existence. All these general characteristics are reflected in Dante's writings after 1302, and the experience of exile imparted a restless urgency to his reflections on his own life and his creative work. The vicissitudes of Dante's political fortune determined the direction of his political interests and the movements of the barometer of hope and despair. For the rest of his life politics was always to be an important factor in his attitude to man and the universe. The very meagre evidence which we have about Dante's own actions must therefore be filled out by conjecture based on our knowledge of the general political background.

For a few years after the coup of 1301 the exiled Whites controlled parts of Tuscany and had the alliance of the nearby city of Pistoia and the sympathy of Bologna. In the end, however, they were unsuccessful. Black Florence, helped by the kingdom of Naples, was too strong for them. In July 1304, a White attempt to break into the city failed, and in April 1306 Pistoia surrendered to Florence. Subsequently, Black rule at Florence was fairly secure. After 1306 the hope of return from exile could not be seriously entertained. What remained was the traditional disposition of parties in Tuscany: Guelf Florence and its allies maintaining the traditional state of suspicious rivalry or intermittent war with the Ghibelline states like Arezzo and Pisa. In these circumstances the White Guelf party withered away. Its remaining adherents could find sympathy and support only among Ghibellines.

Beyond Tuscany dramatic events of European importance were taking place which were to influence Dante's political destiny and to play a large part in his imagination. Although Pope Boniface's intervention in Tuscany in 1301 had been accomplished for him by a French prince, a bitter dispute developed soon after this between the pope and the French king, Philip IV. In 1303 a French expedition in alliance with local enemies of the pope took Boniface prisoner at the seat of his family at Anagni, not far from Rome. Boniface, who was elderly, died a few weeks after this blow to his prestige and confidence. His successor, Benedict XI, introduced a new policy to attempt to pacify the quarrels between the supporters and enemies of Boniface. Owing to the hostility of the Blacks, he failed. His early death was then followed by a long conclave, leading to the election in 1305 of a Gascon, the archbishop of Bordeaux, as Clement V. The new pope never left France and the papacy during his lifetime fell increasingly under French control. The 'Avignon Papacy' – the long period when the popes resided in France – had begun. Philip IV used his new control over the pope to exact a full retribution for the injuries which he believed he had received from Boniface VIII.

In the early years of Clement V's pontificate, papal policy in central Italy was very largely a continuation of that practised by Benedict XI. It was not based, as Boniface's policy had been, on a close alliance with the Guelf powers, especially the Blacks of Florence, but on an attempt to safeguard the integrity of the papal state by bringing Guelfs and Ghibellines to terms with each other. During the years 1304–9 a White or a Ghibelline would have regarded the papacy as a benevolent power. This phase of political history lasted until the election of a new king of the Romans, Henry VII, in 1309.

Dante's movements during these years can be reconstructed only very sketchily. He first associated himself actively with the White Guelf forces outside Florence. He then probably withdrew from Tuscany in 1304 or soon after, but what happened to him after that is very obscure indeed. It is likely that he was dependent on the patronage of the Ghibelline lords with whom he associated. He exchanged poems with Cino da Pistoia, a distinguished Ghibelline lawyer who worked in Pistoia and then, like Dante an exile, in Bologna. In the poems and prose of this period Cino replaced Guido Cavalcanti, who died in 1300, as the poet with whom Dante most closely associated himself and claimed friendship. Later biographers suggest, plausibly enough, though without any hard evidence to support them, that he studied at Bologna. However, practically nothing is certain except that, as he tells us himself, he wandered widely in Italy. Least of all are we able to imagine with any confidence the conditions in which he composed intricate poetry and learned philosophical writings, hardly possible without access to textbooks.

Though the biographical events are obscure, the literary production of the years between 1302 and 1309 was rich and exceedingly complex. In all probability this was the period in which the first part of the *Comedy, Inferno*, was conceived and in which a substantial part of it was written. This will be the subject of the next chapter. We are now concerned with two prose treatises which appear to have been composed entirely in this period: *De Vulgari Eloquentia* (On Vernacular Expression) in Latin, probably written in 1303–4, and *Conv* in Italian, probably written between 1304 and 1308. *DVE* is a defence of the Italian language and a treatise on Italian poetry. *Conv* is a commentary on three allegorical or philosophical poems which Dante had written in the 1290s. Both books are in a sense apologetic literary self-criticism, the writings of a man whose claim to respect and standing in a hostile world is based primarily on his past achievement as a poet, which had made him famous before political misfortune struck him down, and who is therefore determined to defend the nobility and validity of his writings against detractors. But in

Conv the commentary on his poetry ranges so far afield that we are presented in effect with a sketch of a philosophy, a view of man and nature. It is the first of two general statements of a philosophical vision in Dante's writings. The other will be found later in *Paradiso*, the third part of *Comedy*, and the comparison of them embraces many of the main elements in Dante's mature intellectual evolution.

The neoplatonic hierarchy

Conv is divided into four 'treatises', the first mainly a defence of the use of Italian, as against Latin, for a philosophical commentary on Italian poetry. It is linked with the concern to defend the dignity of Italian poetry which led to the composition of *DVE*, in which, with a symmetrical contrast, the status of Italian poetry was enhanced by its being accorded the compliment of analysis in *Latin*. The other three are commentaries on three of the poems of the 1290s which have already been discussed in Chapter 1. The first poem, *Voi ch'intendendo il terzo ciel movete* ('O you who move the third heaven by intellection'), describes Dante's reactions to the Lady who replaced Beatrice. The Lady, we are now told, is the Lady Philosophy. The circles of the heavens, that is the concentric parts of the heavenly bodies, stand for the sciences, and the love which reconciled him to the Lady is the study of those sciences. The second *canzone* or 'song', *Amor che ne la mente mi regiona* ('Love speaking in my mind'), is a panegyric, a poem of praise of the lady. The allegory in this case is about Philosophy as an intermediary between God and man. The third *canzone*, *Le dolci rime d'amor* ('The sweet love-poetry'), as we have seen earlier, is a plainly philosophical poem. The commentary is about its obvious subject: the true nature of human nobility.

Conv was planned to consist of fifteen treatises. The four which Dante wrote contain a sprawling mass of observations on many subjects, extending far beyond the needs of the commentary and set down with no systematic principle of organisation except their, often rather tenuous, relevance to the topics to which the commentary led him. This structure makes the arguments of *Conv* difficult to follow. It results from the dual purpose which Dante tells us he had in writing the book: 'the fear of infamy and the desire to teach' (I ii 15). *Conv* was intended to be both a defence of his poetry and a work of vulgarisation. In its second purpose it was original and ambitious. Dante directed his book explicitly to the many Italian readers who knew no Latin. The enterprise of making the learning of the university masters – normally written down only in Latin – available to the Italian reader had not been attempted on such a scale before. Dante showed in this the strong sense of the potentialities of the Italian language which he discussed more fully in *DVE*, and an awareness of a wide lay audience ready to receive such works. The two purposes – literary criticism and education – clashed. *Conv* was never finished and was not very widely read, but as a picture of a stage in Dante's intellectual evolution it is of the first importance.

Conv reveals, for the first time in Dante's works, an extensive acquaintance with thirteenth-century university thought. We have already noticed, in connection with the philosophy of courtly love, some of the difficulties raised by the use of the works of Aristotle and the non-Christian commentaries of Averroes on Aristotle. By Dante's day a vast literature of commentary and exposition had grown up around Aristotle's books. In the European universities his ideas encountered the bedrock of biblical doctrine on matters like immortality, the creation of the world and revelation. They also encountered a strong neo-platonic tradition and ideas, derived from earlier Christian writers like St. Augustine and Boethius, which emphasised spiritual forces emanating from God and ruling the world, in a manner which was quite difficult to reconcile with Aristotle's cosmology. To hold St Augustine and Aristotle within one consistent system of ideas was in principle an impossible exercise, which nevertheless had to be attempted. Thirteenth-century universities produced a mass of writings, which proposed varying solutions to the problems posed by this multiplicity of authorities.

The centre of this activity was Paris, and among the thinkers who taught there were two leading Dominican friars whose works certainly exerted an influence on Dante. Albertus Magnus was the first to attempt a comprehensive adaptation of Aristotle's natural science for modern use and is one of the main sources of Dante's ideas in that field. St. Thomas Aquinas' most famous writings, the *Summa Contra Gentiles* (Compendium against the Gentiles) and the *Summa Theologiae* (Compendium of Theology), with which Dante probably had some acquaintance, were both attempts by a theologian at a deliberate reconciliation of Aristotelian philosophy and Christian doctrine. Aquinas was a bitter enemy of the Averroist emphasis on Aristotle's materialism, which had been expressed, as we have seen, in Cavalcanti's poetry. The aim of *Conv* was to give the layman a glimpse of the vast body of ideas contained in university philosophy. Dante did not, however, pretend to have a professional or up-to-date acquaintance with that body of ideas himself. He aspired only to be an intermediary giving expression to an enthusiasm.

The aspect of Dante's outlook which emerges most clearly from *Conv* is his very high estimate of the practice of rational philosophy as the means of realising human potentialities. To compress his argument to a brief outline, Dante is saying that, because it is man's essential nature to be rational, the practice of rational speculation will give him the greatest fulfilment. The point of the allegory of the Lady Philosophy is that she acts as an intermediary between the purely spiritual and rational world of the angels and God, on the one hand, and the half material world of man on the other. The human intellect is incapable of rising to the comprehension of rational, non-material beings, that is angels (*Conv* III iv 9), because man exists at a certain point on a scale of being which descends from God at the top to inanimate matter at the bottom. According to their degree of spirituality, creatures are more or less capable of receiving and comprehending the 'divine goodness' – in a physical analogy, objects are more or less capable of being illuminated by radiated light according to how diaphanous they are. On this scale, which is continuous, men in general are the next down from the angels and the next up from animals, so that individual men may be almost angelic or almost brutish. Philosophy contains truths which embody divine wisdom but are also accessible to the human rational intelligence (*Conv* III vii). Rational speculation or contemplation therefore has a special importance for man in enabling him to fulfil his natural potentialities and reach upwards towards higher levels of being.

At the time he wrote *Conv*, Dante was obsessively concerned with the primacy of rational speculation. When he wrote the commentary on the *canzone* about nobility he showed himself to be less interested in 'nobility' itself, a pre-conditioning quality of soul which was the cause of particular virtue, than in the Aristotelian distinction between the active and contemplative life as alternative ways of attaining felicity on earth. The Aristotelian dualism was taken to be equivalent to the Christian distinction between active and contemplative lives.

We have in this life two felicities, according to two roads, good and best, that lead there: the one is the active, the other the contemplative. Although one can attain a good felicity by the active way, the contemplative leads to a better felicity and beatitude, following the proof of the Philosopher in Ethics Book 10. And Christ affirmed it with his own mouth in Luke's gospel. (*Conv* IV xvii 9–10)

Christ's affirmation is his speech to Martha and Mary, signifying traditionally the active and contemplative lives. The poems about the Lady Philosophy are panegyrics of the contemplative life.

The body of teaching with which a philosopher ought to have been familiar was contained in the sciences, whose characteristics Dante described at some length in explaining the allegorical significance of the circles of the heavens in his poem. Starting from the bottom, he equated the first seven heavens with the trivium and quadrivium, the basic subjects of medieval education: grammar, dialectic, rhetoric, arithmetic, music, geometry and astrology. The eighth heaven, the heaven of the stars, was equivalent to physics and metaphysics. The ninth heaven, the *Primo mobile* (Crystalline heaven), corresponds to moral philosophy or ethics. The point of this analogy is that the Crystalline heaven, the highest moving circle, controls by its influence the movements of all the lower circles. Similarly, ethics has a general power over all the other sciences because it directs the minds of men to the study of them. Beyond the Crystalline heaven is the Empyrean, which incorporates the Christian heaven and which is unmoving. This appropriately corresponds to theology which is the study of changeless truth, allowing no conflict of opinion, unlike the other sciences, which allow for diversity of opinion and can therefore be equated with the moving parts of the universe.

But the 'philosophy' which the Lady allegorically represents is not to be equated with the sciences. It was an activity or a state of mind rather than a body of doctrine – what men were led to by study of the sciences. Although for Dante as for other men of his age Aristotle was 'the Philosopher', he did not mean by philosophy the teaching of Aristotle, but also included in the term a Christian significance. He takes the word 'philosophy' to mean etymologically 'love of wisdom' (*Conv* III xi 5), and this could be held to refer to the wisdom of Solomon as well as the wisdom of Aristotle. The fact that it is 'love' of wisdom signifies that the practice of philosophy is also a channel of love between God and man (*Conv* III xii). Philosophy therefore has implications which are religious and extend beyond rational analysis. In one enthusiastic passage, Dante seems to be representing the pagan philosophers of antiquity as thinkers whose efforts in some sense promote not only secular rationality but also the theological truths of Christianity. He thinks that Aristotle and other ancient philosophers were ascetics totally devoted to the pursuit of philosophical truth 'and therefore it is evident that the divine virtue in the form of an angel descends on men in this love'. The pursuit of philosophy finally carries its practitioner – Dante seems to be saying – beyond human reason:

As with her help much is perceived rationally which without her appears marvellous, so with her help it becomes credible that every miracle can be rational in a higher intellect and therefore can exist. From this our good faith has its origin, from which arises the hope of our desire for what we foresee, and thus the work of charity is born. By these three virtues we rise to philosophise in that celestial Athens where the Stoics and Peripatetics and Epicureans harmoniously agree in one will by the light of eternal truth. (*Conv* III xiv 14–15)

Dante posits here that the practice of philosophy can make men aware of the existence of truths beyond the ordinary conclusions of human reason, and therefore provide a basis for the theological virtues of faith, hope and charity. He apparently sees the work of pagan philosophers as both converging on Christian doctrine and actually providing a basis for it.

But Dante's view of the relationship between rational and religious truths is finally equivocal. The speculative power, he says at one point, cannot be perfected in this life, as its full use would involve the possession of God, who can be known in this life only in the sense that his effects are known. Dante reinforces this argument with an allegorical interpretation of the gospel story of the three Marys who went to find the body of Jesus at his tomb. They were met by an angel in white who told them that

Jesus had gone, but said they should tell the disciples to go to Galilee and find him there. In Dante's exposition this means that the 'three sects of the active life, the Epicureans, Stoics and Peripatetics' looked for beatitude in earthly life and failed to find it. The angel in white is nobility granted by God which, instructing humanity by the use of reason, tells him to look for beatitude in speculation. 'Whiteness is a colour more full of corporeal light than any other and contemplation is more full of spiritual light than anything else here below.' So beatitude is attainable 'as if imperfect' in the active life and 'as if perfect' in the contemplative life. 'These two are the most direct ways leading to the highest beatitude, which one cannot have here, as appears indeed in what has been said' (*Conv* IV xxii 11–18). The conclusion is ambiguous. An earthly beatitude dependent on reason has been promised but is said to be necessarily incomplete. The philosophers appear to have been displaced as guides to beatitude by the angelic emissaries of God. Dante does not seem to have wanted to work out a rigorous distinction between the spheres of reason and revelation.

Dante's conception of the significance of philosophy was dependent as we have seen on his view that everything in the universe proceeds from the divinity and contains something of the divine nature – more or less according to its distance from the godhead and the fineness of the materials of which it is made. The universe is held together by the love joining its parts, of which human loves and desires are an aspect.

The goodness of God is received in one way by substances separated [from matter], that is Angels, which have no material grossness but are almost diaphanous through the purity of their form; differently by the human soul which, although it is in part free from matter is in part impeded like a man under water except for his head and thus not entirely in or out of it; differently again by animals, whose soul is made entirely of matter but somewhat ennobled; by plants; by minerals; differently from all these by the earth which is the most material and therefore the most remote from and disproportioned to the first, simplest and noblest virtue which is entirely intellectual, that is God. (*Conv* III vii 5)

The essence of the view of the universe, which Dante had developed under the influence of fragments of neoplatonic thought, was that the Godhead was pure, spiritual light. The highest beings in the universe were the most simple, the most spiritual and the most uniform. The lower parts of creation were increasingly diverse and material. The tendency of this picture of the universe was to blunt the characteristic Christian distinction between God on the one hand and creation on the other, made by Him but separate. Within this general framework it was consistent that, having stressed the importance of man's rationality as the aspect of his nature which fixed him in a particular position in the scale of being, the tendency of Dante's picture of man should be to enlarge his capacity to comprehend ultimate truths, by the use of his rational intellect, without irrational revelation.

The conception of a hierarchy of being emanating from God was not merely an abstract idea. It was the principle according to which the universe was ordered, and it was manifested in the organisation of matter and space in the astronomical world as Dante conceived of it. Treatise II of *Conv* contains a description of the heavens as a background to the *canzone, Voi ch'intendendo il terzo ciel movete*, which literally attributes the growth of love to the influence of the planet Venus and allegorically equates the circles of the heavens with the sciences. Dante here took the opportunity to describe the layout of the universe, and in particular the revolutions of the heavenly bodies. Starting from the bottom, that is from the circle nearest to earth, the circles of the heavens are: 1 Moon, 2 Mercury, 3 Venus, 4 Sun, 5 Mars, 6 Jupiter, 7 Saturn, 8 Starry Heaven, 9 Crystalline heaven or *Primo mobile*. All the nine heavens rotate around the earth. Above them is the Empyrean, which does not move. Dante's Empyrean is the Christian heaven, but it is also the soul of the world, formed in the divine mind, the source of influences which radiate throughout the universe. While the Empyrean is still, a place of total rest and completeness, the ninth circle adjoining it, the Crystalline heaven moves very fast because of the desire of each of its parts to be in the closest possible contact with 'that most divine still circle' – the Empyrean. The movements of the heavens are thus powered by love and desire, the intense attractive force of the divine envelope of the physical world. This conception of the relation between Empyrean and Crystalline heaven enables Dante to establish a link between a purely spiritual heaven and the created world: eternity and the material world are joined in one system.

The Crystalline Heaven is transparent, an imagined construction corresponding to no visible heavenly body. It performs two functions: the mathematical function, for which it was invented by Ptolemy, of helping to account for the movements of the celestial bodies below it; and a philosophical function, which appeals particularly to Dante. 'The principles of philosophy ... require of necessity a very simple *primo mobile*' (*Conv* II ii 5), or, in other words, the source of movement in the heavens must, to conform with the hierarchy of being, be simpler and purer than the heavenly bodies below it, which it directs. Below the Crystalline heaven are the heavens of the visible stars, the planets and the moon. Dante cultivated astronomy and displayed considerable technical knowledge of that subject both in the *Comedy* and here in *Conv*. From a general philosophical point of view, however, the most important feature of his account of the heavens is that their movements are governed by affective principles similar to that linking the Crystalline heaven to the Empyrean. Each of the eight lower circles has an equator between its poles. That part of each circle which is closer to the equator 'is more noble by comparison with the poles because it has more movement and actuality, and more life and form, and is more touched by what is above it, and in consequence is more virtuous' (*Conv* II iii 15).

The circles of the heavens are inhabited by angels. These are described by Dante in Aristotelian language as 'substances separate from matter': that is to say they are purely spiritual beings, pure intelligences. They are the 'movers' of the heavens. The rotations of the heavenly bodies take place, not for mechanical reasons, but because of the spiritual activity of angels: 'The circulation of the heavens which is the steering of the world follows the speculation of certain of these, so it is like an ordered civil life perceived in the speculation of the movers' (*Conv* II iv 13). Following a traditional catalogue, Dante divides the hosts of angels into three hierarchies with ascending spiritual powers. Each of the hierarchies is divided into three orders, so that each of the nine circles of the heavens has an order of angels controlling it. They are also intermediaries between the divinity and the earthly world. Susceptible themselves to divine influence, they also exert an influence on earthly events. Dante is a believer in astrology. The attribution of love to the influence of the movers of the circle of Venus is not metaphorical. Though it is given another allegorical meaning, it is meant in itself to be literally acceptable. The star Venus 'because of the nobility of its movers has such virtue that it has very great power over our souls and other things' (*Conv* II vii 10).

Stars also exert an influence over the process of generation and therefore over individual human characters. One of the thorniest problems, with which Dante had to deal in *Conv*, was the process of generation of the human being, body and soul, which he was led to consider because of his contention that nobility was a quality infused into the individual soul by God, and not inherited from biological ancestors. For medieval theorists it was difficult to evolve a satisfactory account of the early development of the human being, which would satisfy the two Christian requirements: firstly, the union of the body with a soul capable of general rationality in life and, secondly, the survival of a unique personal soul after death. Dante believed that the male seed brought with it generative power and also characteristics which came both directly from God and from the influence of the stars. This set in motion the evolution of the soul in the embryo, until it was ready to receive the 'possible intellect' from God. The celestial and other influences, operating at an early stage in life, would produce wide variations in the characters of men. Those who were favourably affected and received a generous share of divine goodness would be capable of almost divine understanding:

There are some of such an opinion that they say, if all the preceding virtues were in agreement at their best disposition in producing a soul, then so much of the deity would descend into it that it would be almost a God incarnate. (*Conv* IV xxi 10)

Behind *Conv* is undoubtedly a considerable amount of reading in the learned authors of antiquity and the Middle Ages, extending far beyond the books by Boethius and Cicero which Dante himself tells us first turned his mind towards philosophy after the death of Beatrice. We have no evidence as to when or how this reading was done: in his youth, when he may have been a serious student; in the period after the death of Beatrice, when he tells us he frequented the schools of the Florentine convents; or in the days of exile. The book reads, however, as though he was communicating live enthusiasms, ideas still molten in his mind. The problem of the sources is a difficult one. It might be expected that many passages of a book like *Conv*, which purports to introduce the ordinary reader to arcane learning, would be easily identifiable as reports of arguments in, say, Aristotle or Aquinas. On the contrary, it is usually difficult to identify Dante's sources even when he has himself told us what they are. We are often left uncertain whether he was following Aristotle or one of the medieval commentators *on* Aristotle, and uncertain whether or not he had read and understood the passage to which he appears to refer.

Among the ancients, Dante refers very frequently to Aristotle and less frequently to Cicero, Boethius and Ptolemy. But the only book of Aristotle which he certainly knew directly was the *Ethics*. The references to other works of Aristotle may be taken from thirteenth-century writers rather than directly from translations of Aristotle himself. He also refers to the *Liber de Causis* (The Book of Causes), a late-antique neoplatonic work, which was popular in medieval Europe. Of modern writers, the most frequently mentioned is St. Thomas Aquinas. Dante shows his respect for the great Dominican theologian by telling us that when he calls his philosophical *canzone* about nobility his 'against-the-erring', he is copying the title of Aquinas's *Summa Contra Gentiles*. He also refers almost as frequently to Albertus Magnus, and to the Arabic philosophers Averroes and Avicenna, and to some of the Arab writers on astronomy. His range of reference is wide but his citations are unreliable, perhaps partly because he made references from memory or at second hand. The most important reason is probably that his imagination was naturally eclectic and poetic. Though he certainly had a good deal of technical knowledge, he constructed a personal philosophical vision which did not clearly follow, either as a whole or, generally, even in particular passages, the argument of a particular authority. Nor does he adhere clearly to a philosophical school. The materials of his learned theories are drawn very widely from the common stock of learning generally available in the arts faculties of the universities, but it is futile to attempt to classify him as a Thomist or an Averroist. Nevertheless, there are some features of Dante's philosophical exposition which indicate distinct intellectual preferences. The most marked is his inclination towards a broadly neoplatonic view of the nature of the universe. Neoplatonism was a powerful influence in thirteenth-century universities, which affected all scholastic thinkers to some degree, although some more than others. Aquinas showed that the neoplatonic *Liber de Causis* was not, as his predecessors commonly believed, by Aristotle, and he took a more critical view of neoplatonism. Dante was clearly attracted by the neoplatonic tradition as he met it in that book and in the scientific works of Albertus Magnus. He tends to see the universe both physically and morally as a graded hierarchy of being held together by divine emanation from the Godhead transmitted through the levels of the hierarchy. In the neoplatonic picture the distinction between God and his creation is relatively under-emphasised and the universe is a harmonious system of spiritual influences. This idea never lost its hold on him. As Beatrice is the great permanent invention of the *VN* period, the neoplatonic universe is the great permanent discovery recorded in *Conv*.

The other feature which distinguishes Dante's outlook in *Conv* is his enthusiastic optimism about the powers of human reason. This is consistent with neoplatonist spiritualism: the spiritual side of man's nature is open to influences from the divine centre because there is a gradation rather than a sharp break between them.

One important passage in *Conv* points forward to other themes elaborated more fully in later works. In the *canzone* on nobility expounded in Treatise IV, the view that nobility results from wealth and ancestry is attributed to a Roman emperor. The opposed view of nobility as an endowment of the individual, is partly drawn from Aristotle's *Ethics*. In *Conv* Dante distinguishes between the authority of Aristotle in philosophical questions and the political authority of the Roman Emperor, to show that the emperor's proper sphere does not include philosophy. Considering the direction of the argument, which is concerned only negatively with the Roman empire, the empire receives a very generous amount of space. This passage (*Conv* IV iv–v) contains the first indication, largely irrelevant to the main argument of this part of *Conv*, that Dante believed in an all-powerful worldwide empire. Following Aristotle – his argument runs – man's proper development of his powers requires that he should live in a State; but warfare between States remains an obstacle to felicity. It is logically necessary therefore to have a single world-monarchy. The Roman emperors are destined by divine providence to fill this role. The conjunction of the birth of Jesus with the foundation of the Empire showed that it was divinely planned to prepare for the spread of Christianity. It is likely that his interest in these ideas was founded on the bitter experience of strife in divided Italy and on attachment to the Ghibelline party which advocated imperial power – at a very low ebb in the first decade of the fourteenth century, owing to the failure of Albert of Austria, King of the Romans, to interest himself in Italian politics. The imperialist angle on politics would have been unlikely to attract the citizen of Guelf Florence. Dante was probably first introduced to this line of thought by the associations which he formed after 1302.

The passage on the Roman empire in *Conv* also reveals a new poetic star of the first magnitude in Dante's heaven: Virgil, the author of the *Aeneid*, which told of Aeneas's wanderings leading to the foundation of Rome. The exaltation of Virgil is common enough in the Middle Ages, but the special significance which Dante came to attach to him probably developed after his exile. The enthusiasm for imperialism and the enthusiasm for Virgil, the pagan celebrator of Rome's imperial mission, arose at the same time. It must have been about this time also that Dante was conceiving and nurturing the idea of the first part of the *Comedy*, *Inferno*, the book in which he was to imitate Aeneas' journey into the underworld under Virgil's guidance.

3 Hell

The Divine Comedy *as a whole*

The *Comedy* is the most carefully wrought and the most precisely and intricately symmetrical of great literary works. Everything, from the careful balance of episodes and personages and the meticulously respected time-sequence of the fictional journey through the other world to the uniformity of poetic structure, suggests a perfectly finished and consistent work of art. But for the reader who attempts to go beyond the exterior enjoyment of this magnificent artifice to understand its meaning and its relation to Dante's ideas, it presents an ocean of problems. The *Comedy* was probably composed over a period of not less than fifteen years, during which period Dante passed through some dramatic vicissitudes, and some of his basic ideas and interests probably changed substantially. The dates of composition of the three parts of the *Comedy* are all quite uncertain, as is the degree of revision: we can only conjecture how much *Inf* was revised to conform with *Para*. The three parts contain hundreds of references to contemporary personalities and incidents whose significance for Dante is often obscure to us. The conception of the *Comedy* was original and remained unique, so that there are no self-evident critical standards of comparison. There are, therefore, serious uncertainties, not merely about the interpretation of particular passages, but also about the kind of poetry that Dante intended to write, in particular what kind of allegorical messages the surface story conceals. All these reasons make it hazardous to attempt an interpretation of Dante's evolution through the period of the *Comedy*.

The *Comedy* consists of three main sections, each usually called a *cantica*: *Inferno*, *Purgatorio* and *Paradiso*. Each of the three sections is divided into cantos, of varying length but all made up of three-line stanzas. After the introductory canto, each part consists of thirty-three cantos – in all three times thirty-three plus one, which makes a hundred. This numerical symmetry and preference for the number three, the number of the Trinity and of the realms of the other world, is characteristic. The three *cantiche* relate to the story of Dante's journey through Hell, Purgatory and Paradise. *Para* is different from the other two, because for most of it Dante is not actually journeying through 'Paradise' but through the circles of the planets and stars towards Heaven. *Inf* and *Purg* are mostly set in Hell and Purgatory. The physical setting of the entire journey is determined by Dante's view of cosmology. Hell is a funnel concentrically below Jerusalem on the earth's surface and extending to the centre of the earth. The mount of Purgatory rises out of the southern hemisphere, directly opposite. *Inf* and *Purg* thus describe a journey through the earth's centre, ending at the Earthly Paradise on the summit of the mount of Purgatory. *Para* is a journey through the circles of the heavenly bodies, concentrically outside the earth, as described in *Conv*, ending in the Empyrean. The journey takes place in Holy Week 1300. Dante maintains this fiction meticulously, by precise references to the disposition of the heavenly bodies as they would have been in that week at various points on the journey. Thus it can be calculated that the journey down through Hell extends from nightfall on Good Friday evening 1300 until Saturday evening. The climb out of Hell to the other side of the earth takes until Easter Sunday. Four days are spent in Ante-Purgatory, climbing the mount of Purgatory and in the Earthly Paradise at its summit; one day in rising through the circles of the heavens to the Empyrean, where he finally reaches the Godhead. He undertakes this journey with the help of guides: he is taken into Hell and through it by the Roman poet, Virgil, who has been sent by Beatrice, herself an inhabitant of Heaven. Virgil also then takes him up the mount of Purgatory to the threshold of the Earthly Paradise, where he disappears, to be replaced by Beatrice herself as guide. She takes him up through the heavenly circles to the Empyrean, where she gives place in the final cantos to St. Bernard, the great twelfth-century abbot of Clairvaux and mystical writer. During the journey, Virgil and then Beatrice explain the significance of the various sections of Hell, Purgatory and Paradise through which they pass. In these domains, Dante meets a large number of spirits and is enlightened, either by his guides or by the spirits themselves, about the actions in the terrestrial world by which they have merited the fate of being consigned to punishment in one of the circles of Hell, or allowed to expiate their fault in Purgatory, or have been granted a place with the re-deemed. In conformity with his careful preservation of the fiction, Dante includes only spirits of people who were dead before Easter 1300. References to events after that date, though they are very common, are always in the form of prophecy.

The first problem which arises in an interpretation of the *Comedy* is the extent to which we ought to assume uniformity and unity. Was Dante executing a single plan, so that each part of the poem has a preconceived place in the development of a general theme, which embraces them all? Or was he fitting together passages composed under the influence of different, un-connected inspirations which eventually found places within a single framework? The suggestions of patchwork composition make the question inescapable. Firstly, there are the differences between the *cantiche*. Much of *Para* – however sublime the poetry in which it is expressed – can be read as a theoretical treatise on philosophical and theological matters. *Inf* is about the failings of fallen humanity and their just punishment, with a strong bias towards the contemporary Italian political world. The difference is not just that one is about Hell and the other about Paradise. They seem to be inspired by a quite different focus of interest, and though they are, of course, linked by Dante's journey and the patronage of Beatrice, it is not difficult to imagine them as independent works. Secondly, there are the passages within the *cantiche* which seem to have an independent life of their own. For example, the encounter with Ulysses in *Inf* or the speech of Justinian in *Para* are set pieces which, however well they are fitted in, do not seem to have an absolutely necessary function at that particular point in the unfolding of the whole design. It is possible, therefore, to regard the *Comedy* as representing a suc-cession of different preoccupations of Dante at different times, over a long period. The three *cantiche* are, to some extent, sep-arable works and contain passages which are easily isolated, yet they are knit together by the guides, by the progressive unfolding of the nature of the other world and by the autobiographical account of Dante's own destiny. But it is a matter for specu-lation, especially in the case of *Inf*, how far the unifying features were superimposed in later revisions some time after the *cantica* had been conceived and largely composed. Reading *Inf* alone, it is possible to imagine that Beatrice might have been introduced at a late stage. The conception of his own destiny, which Dante expresses enigmatically in the prologue canto and in *Para*, is not altogether easy to square with the impression conveyed by *Inf* as a whole. These problems will be taken up when *Para* is reached.

The problem of unity and diversity is bound up with that of dating. *Para* was certainly written at the end of Dante's life, but there is no certain evidence about the composition of *Inf* and *Purg*. Theories about their dating depend very largely on detailed analysis of the dates of events referred to, but they are complicated and speculative because they have to take account of the possibility of a main period of composition, followed by a later revision. A probable view, favoured by recent scholarship, is that *Inf* was written about 1304–8 and *Purg* about 1308–13; they were then revised and in places brought up to date, *Para* being composed after 1314. It must be admitted that this is hypothetical and that other very different opinions – for instance that the whole poem was composed after 1312 or that it was begun before 1302 – have been held. The hypothesis of composition in three stages, 1304–8, 1308–13 and 1314–21, has, however, the enormous advantage that it allows a rational account of Dante's evolution to be constructed in which the subject-matter of the three *cantiche* can be shown – again hypothetically of course – to have an intelligible relationship to a possible development of Dante's ideas.

The largest uncertainty which faces the reader when he tries to interpret the *Comedy* concerns the use of allegory. In a letter which he wrote towards the end of his life to his great patron, Can Grande della Scala, the lord of Verona, accompanying a gift of part of *Para*, Dante offered the following guidance to his patron in reading the whole *Comedy*:

It must be understood that the meaning of this work is not of one kind only; rather the work may be described as 'polysemous', that is, having several meanings; for the first meaning is that which is conveyed by the letter, and the next is that which is conveyed by what the letter signifies; the former of which is called literal, while the latter is called allegorical or mystical, . . . The subject then of the whole work, taken in the literal sense only, is the state of souls after death, pure and simple. For on and about that the argument of the whole work turns. If however the work be regarded from the allegorical point of view, the subject is man according as by his merits or demerits in the exercise of his free will he is deserving of reward or punishment by justice.

The authenticity of the letter to Can Grande has been questioned. Some scholars hold that it was composed after Dante's death by someone who wanted to give the *Comedy* an inoffensive meaning which would make it acceptable to ecclesiastical authorities. This is a scholarly puzzle which, like some other problems posed by Dante's works, will probably never be solved. A writer on Dante has, at least provisionally, to take one side or the other. The view adopted here is that the letter is probably genuine and provides helpful information on Dante's intentions. What it says at this point is, in any case, clearly true: the description of the spirits whom Dante meets in the other world carries implications, which are not always clearly stated, about the moral significance of the type of behaviour which they exemplify. Dante gives no further general allegorical interpretation of the *Comedy,* so we are left to speculate about the further implication, if any, of his statement in the letter. He does, however, make one other point in the same passage: that is to remind the reader of the normal medieval practice of biblical exegesis, in which texts were given, in addition to their literal meaning, an 'allegorical', a 'moral', and an 'anagogical' (or 'mystical') meaning. The example which he uses is Psalm 114, 'When Israel went out of Egypt . . .', of which he says:

For if we consider the letter alone, the thing signified to us is the going out of the children of Israel from Egypt in the time of Moses; if the allegory, our redemption through Christ is signified; if the moral sense, the conversion of the soul from the sorrow and misery of sin to a state of grace is signified; if the anagogical, the passing of the sanctified soul from the bondage of the corruption of this world to the liberty of everlasting glory is signified.

That passage from the Bible is actually used in the *Comedy* (*Purg* II 46). In Ante-Purgatory Dante sees a shipful of souls arriving to begin the ascent of Purgatory. As they approach the shore they are singing Psalm 114. The psalm would be meaningless if it were not taken to have the unspoken significance attributed to it in Dante's letter: that the souls were celebrating the opportunity for redemption offered by Christ's sacrifice, and the existence of Purgatory, and their escape from the bondage of terrestrial life. There are a great many references to the Bible in the *Comedy*, which, it must always be assumed, are invested with a similar kind of allegorical significance. In a rather less conventional fashion, but certainly not one without precedent, Dante also attributed moral significance to personalities and incidents drawn from pagan history. On the same shore, at the foot of Purgatory, Dante and Virgil meet the Roman hero Cato the Younger, who – surprisingly since he was both a pagan and a suicide – fills the role of guardian of the entrance to Purgatory. Dante knew that Cato was a man of high principle, a believer in immortality who had chosen to die rather than submit to Caesar. Though the fictional Dante (as he appears in his own poem) has only the day before seen the souls of Caesar's traitorous murderers devoured eternally by Satan in the bottommost pit of Hell, he now finds another enemy of Caesar, exalted into a position of divine trust because he had chosen honourable death rather than dishonourable life. The supreme exercise of free will makes him a fitting guardian of Purgatory, in which the soul must exercise its will to overcome sin. Dante tended to use all his characters, biblical or pagan, for moral purposes, with the difference that the Bible carried traditional significances which he could hardly escape, while the pagan world was a freer field for invention. This catholicity was encouraged by the general significance which Dante had come by this time to attribute to Roman history as a succession of events, parallel with the history of the Jews, and, like the events of the Old Testament, providentially directed towards the Incarnation and Christianity. This view of the equal and parallel significance of ecclesiastical plus Old Testament history on the one hand, and imperial plus classical history on the other, led Dante to invest sacred and profane events with parallel metaphorical significance. In doing this he was adding a particular systematic arrangement to a general medieval attitude to past events.

It must always be assumed, then, that the characters and events of the *Comedy* are 'polysemous', that they incorporate more or less complex patterns of meaning which are not stated but have to be inferred. However much one knows about Dante's sources and the intellectual traditions which were familiar to him, the interpretation remains speculative. This is, of course, in a sense no more than is true of all poetry, but the need of interpretation is unusually heightened in the *Comedy*, partly because it teems with people drawn from ancient and recent history, and partly because Dante is presenting an intricate moral argument through the portrayal of historical personages. Elaborate commentaries for puzzled readers were being prepared within a very few years of Dante's death. The greatest uncertainty of interpretation, however, relates to the major unifying themes in the story, rather than to particular episodes; especially to the three main characters, Virgil, Beatrice and Dante himself. Virgil is ostensibly the shade of the Roman poet sent by the agency of Beatrice from his place in Limbo to conduct Dante through Hell and Purgatory. Beatrice is the spirit of Dante's old love of the *VN*, a redeemed spirit who descends from heaven to conduct Dante through the spheres. How far do these characters, like the Lady of the *Conv* poems, 'stand for' something else? The most common interpretations have been that Virgil stands for human reason, Beatrice for Divine Grace. And linked with this is the question of Dante's own soul. Is his journey through Hell, Purgatory and Heaven an allegory for the progress of a human soul through stages of understanding or stages of conversion? Explanations of this kind have been common among the commentators. There is no explicit warrant for them either in the *Comedy* itself or in the letter to Can Grande, and they have thus to be treated with reserve. An elaborate colouring of poetic significance is attached to the three characters and expressed in many details – Virgil *is* a great pagan and, therefore, endowed with understanding within the limits of reason; Beatrice *is* endowed with the understanding of the blessed spirits and, therefore, knows what only they know; Dante *does* progress through many experiences from confusion to Christian knowledge. This attachment of significance to the character does not, however, imply a systematic allegory.

Although the allegorical element is important and pervasive, one of the most striking and novel features of the *Comedy*, particularly of *Inf*, is a certain kind of personal realism. Many of Dante's characters are, of course, legendary or historical figures of antiquity. But many others are people whom Dante knew or figures of the recent past whose characteristics were well known to him and to his contemporaries. The insignificant Florentine,

Ciacco, who appears as a glutton in *Inf* VI to give Dante a preview of the next two years of Florentine history, was, as Boccaccio, the great Florentine story-teller of the generation following Dante's tells us, a well-known glutton and sponger in real life. Though otherwise unknown to written history, he was presumably a city character whom readers, Florentine readers at least, would have recognised, very likely with amusement, as a suitable choice for a deflating commentator on Florentine politics. In the circle of the lustful (*Inf* V), in perhaps the best-known episode in the *Inf*, Dante meets two lovers, Paolo and Francesca, two spirits borne on the wind, eternally together but eternally separated in punishment for their sin. In reply to Dante's inquiry, Francesca explains how she came to commit adultery with Paolo through the lust aroused in them by reading together the story of Lancelot and Guinevere. Dante himself read how Lancelot took the first guilty kiss from Guinevere in a French version of the Arthurian legend. It is a powerful piece of erotic romanticism. In this episode elements of the Lancelot story are taken over, and the pathos is intensified by the addition of the fact that they are condemned to eternal damnation for their sin. It may also be read as Dante's wistful but condemnatory valediction to the ethos of courtly love poetry, which had dominated his own youthful writing. These significant meanings are, however, attached to two characters who were also real people. Francesca was a lady of the Polenta family of Ravenna, with which Dante became acquainted during his exile. She was married to Gianciotto Malatesta of Rimini, whose brother, the Paolo of the story with whom she committed adultery so that her husband slew them both, held the post of Capitano at Florence in 1282 when Dante was seventeen. Dante may even be recalling some youthful shared interest in romantic literature. In any case, he is talking about a real scandal, which had happened about twenty years before he wrote, and he is quite likely to have met at least one of the characters. This is something very different from a story about mythical figures like Lancelot and Guinevere. Dante was no doubt encouraged to the portrayal of real people by the Bible and the *Aeneid*, but to populate Hell with genuine contemporaries, exhibiting their known actions and characteristics as archetypal failings of human nature, required a leap of the imagination. This probably owes a good deal to the customs of

Florentine city life, in which the realistic presentation of real people in comic poetry (like Dante's own exchange with Forese Donati), in prose stories and in political chronicles was relatively highly developed. These were characteristics of the life of the Italian commune and pre-eminently of Florence. Personal realism, encouraged by the intense egalitarian intercourse of city life, is a much more peculiar feature of Dante's art than the penchant for symbolism and allegory, which he shares with the medieval world in general. Dante's mature imagination, therefore, combines an extreme abstractness of general conception with an extreme concreteness of personal representation. Clearly focused individuals are set against the abstract pattern of the whole universe. Because of its crowds of characters, *Inf*, of all Dante's works, is the one in which the Florentine turbulence, 'the new people and the quick profits', to use his own phrase, in contrast with the hieratic forms of medieval philosophy and kingship, which also fascinated him, is most strongly present.

Inferno

The prologue to the *Comedy* finds Dante lost in a wood at the foot of a hill, weary from the journey of his life, and faced by three frightening beasts: a leopard, usually taken to be a symbol of lust, a lion, symbolising pride, and a she-wolf, symbolising avarice. He is rescued by the shade of Virgil, who tells him that the wolf will be irresistible until a mysterious saviour, the 'Veltro', comes, but that he, Virgil, will show Dante another way, through Hell. After some persuasion by Virgil, who explains that he is an emissary of Beatrice, they finally enter Hell to begin the journey in canto III. The rest of *Inf* is taken up with their journey together down through Hell, past sinners guilty of crimes of increasing wickedness, until they reach Satan himself in the lowest pit.

The model which gave Dante the idea of *Inf* was Virgil's *Aeneid*, Book VI. The *Aeneid* tells the story of Aeneas after leaving Troy when it was destroyed by the Greeks, until he settled in Italy, to become the ancestor of the Romans, in the course of which journey he visited the underworld. Virgil's underworld has many resemblances to Dante's Hell. Visitors to it have to be ferried across Acheron, a river in Hell, by Charon. Its upper and lower regions are divided by a forbidding fortification (equivalent to the walled city of Dis in Dante, *Inf* VIII), beyond which sinners are punished appropriately for various crimes. Before he reaches this inner region, Aeneas discourses with the shades of figures from his earlier life: Palinurus, his drowned helmsman and Dido Queen of Carthage whom he had loved and abandoned. The Virgilian and Dantean other worlds diverge when Aeneas passes on into the Elysian fields and to the dialogue with the shade of his father, Anchises, in which the history of Rome is foretold. Dante has an interview with his ancestor, Cacciaguida, in *Para*, which is reminiscent of Anchises' speech, but in general Purgatory and Paradise owe little to Virgil. In *Inf*, however, there is a general parallelism, not only in the physical arrangements and in many poetic details, but in the general idea of Hell as a place where punishment can be observed and also where the shades of the friendly dead can be interrogated about their fate. The inspiration for *Inf*, and very likely the inspiration for the whole *Comedy*, arose out of Dante's enthusiasm for Virgil.

Virgil himself dominates *Inf* as Dante's guide. Why was he chosen for the central role? In order to make him a knowledgeable guide Dante probably had to invent a legend that he had once been sent down that way by a sorceress. Virgil is greeted in the first place as Dante's literary hero and inspiration

> Tu se' lo mio maestro e 'l mio autore,
> tu se solo colui da cu' io tolsi
> lo bello stilo che m'ha fatto onore.
>
> You are my master and my author,
> You alone are he from whom I took
> the fair style which has gained me honour.
>
> (*Inf* I 85–7)

Dante took over from his medieval predecessors the idea, based on his supposed prediction of the incarnation in the fourth Eclogue, that Virgil was not only a great poet but also a great prophet. But more important than this for Dante was the more obvious fact that Virgil had portrayed the revelation of Rome's history to Aeneas in the course of a journey into the underworld such as Dante himself was now to undertake.

By this journey of which you [Virgil] give an account, He [Aeneas] learned things which were the cause of his victory [leading to the establishment of Rome] and of the papal mantle. (*Inf* II 25–7)

Book VI of the *Aeneid* with its dual importance as a record of a journey in the underworld to meet the souls of the dead and a revelation of Aeneas' imperial destiny was what made Virgil important to Dante. Virgil was Dante's guide both in literature and in Ghibelline politics, the source of conceptions which gave meaning both to his art and his politics in the years of exile.

Virgil explains the structure of Hell to Dante in canto XI. At this point in the story the two travellers have already descended through the upper six circles, in which they have encountered, apart from the good pagans in Limbo, sinners undergoing punishment for lust, gluttony, avarice, prodigality, anger and heresy. They pause to look down into a more repulsive area from which a foul stench is rising. Below them, Virgil explains, are three more circles (seven, eight and nine) containing various kinds of sinners whose malice (*malizia*) has caused injustice (*ingiuria*). Malice may work through either force or fraud. Fraud is a capacity peculiar to man, unknown to other creatures, and, therefore, a perversion of man's nature more displeasing to God, so those guilty of it are placed further down than sinners guilty merely of violence. Within this general framework Virgil gives a more detailed analysis of the types of sin. Force may be directed against neighbours (murder and plunder), oneself (suicide and prodigality) or God and Nature (blasphemy and sodomy). Fraud is subdivided into that directed against those who do not repose trust in the sinner (hypocrites, flatterers, sorcerers, thieves, simoniacs, panders, corrupt politicians) and, worst of all, treachery towards the trusting. When the fictional Dante asks humbly how the sinners they have already seen in the first six circles fit into this scheme, Virgil brusquely refers him to the division of the evil dispositions in Aristotle's *Ethics* into three kinds: incontinence, malice and bestiality. Incontinence is less offensive to God: the upper circles contain those guilty merely of lack of self-control, not of ill will.

The plan of Dante's Hell needs an explanation of this kind because it does not conform to any obvious pattern. In contrast to the scheme of sins in Purgatory, which is quite simply the order of the seven cardinal sins recognised in the theology of penitence, the scheme of Hell is both more elaborate and highly eccentric. The Aristotelian pattern adduced by Virgil does not actually fit either: Aristotle does not base a classification on his distinction between incontinence, malice and bestiality, and Dante uses the third category, bestiality, only fleetingly if at all. Some of Dante's terms and conceptions are derived from contemporary scholastic theology. For example, malice and injustice, used as technical terms, and the distinction between injuries to self, another and God are conceptions which can be found in the writings of Aquinas. But the distinction between crimes of violence and crimes of fraud, which is the central principle governing the organisation of the lower circles of hell, was probably taken from one of Cicero's philosophical works, *De Officiis*, where he says that *iniuria* may be done either by force or by fraud, 'both very alien to man, but fraud the more hateful'.

What emerges from this is that Dante made up his own scheme for Hell. It contains echoes of Aristotle, Cicero and Aquinas but, in spite of Virgil's misleading remarks, cannot actually be justified by reference to any or all of them. After passing through Limbo (*Inf* IV) which houses the good but unbaptised pagans, including Aristotle and, normally, Virgil himself, they pass through the circles of the incontinent to the city of Dis, which contains the heretics. Then comes the division between upper and lower Hell. Below are the sinners guilty of malice. The circle of the violent is passed through fairly quickly, the longest time being spent with the crime of sodomy, which highlights Dante's Florentine mentor Brunetto Latini (*Inf* XV–XVI). The rest of the *Inf*, more than half, belongs to the various species of fraud, starting with mere panders and seducers, ending with traitors to their lords, including the supreme traitor, Satan.

The plan of Hell is also explicitly related to the historical degeneracy of the human race. Virgil explains in *Inf* XIV that Crete was in classical legend the cradle of the human race in its days of innocence. Inside Mount Ida in Crete stands a 'great old man' with his face turned towards Rome 'as his mirror'. His head is of gold, his arms and breast of silver, his trunk of brass, his legs of iron, his right foot of clay. This extraordinary figure appears to have been made up by a conflation of the figure in the Old Testament dream of Nebuchadnezzar and the ages of man in

Ovid's *Metamorphoses*. The materials of which the old man is made symbolise the decline of humanity from the innocence of the golden age, the condition of happiness which some ancient writers supposed early men to have enjoyed, the right foot possibly representing the decayed spiritual power as opposed to the healthier temporal empire. Below the golden head he is broken by a 'fissure' from which drip tears which flow down to form the rivers of Hell, Acheron, Styx and Phlegethon. Dante invented his elaborate legend to connect man's fall from terrestrial goodness with the formation of Hell, in which human failings are classified and punished.

Inf can be read from one point of view as a treatise on human sins in verse, the failings of humanity being approached through the observation of their appropriate punishment. Dante expended a great deal of literary ingenuity in devising appropriate punishments to fit crimes, like the soothsayers having their heads firmly turned to look backwards, or, on a grander scale, Satan's hideous triple face mocking his attempt to supplant the triune God. The systematic panorama of human weakness has some connection with preoccupations revealed elsewhere in works of Dante's early exile period. The two great moral *canzoni* written in the period 1302–4, *Tre donne* and *Doglia mi reca* ('Grief makes me bold'), are both bitter comments on contemporary humanity. *Tre donne* complains that men have exiled justice, generosity and temperance from their hearts. *Doglia mi reca* has the strange theme that women should withhold their love from men, because of the decline of virtue: 'Men have cut themselves off from virtue – no not men, but evil beasts in man's likeness. O God, how strange – to choose to fall from master to slave, from life to death.' A rather more specific foreshadowing of the theme of *Inf* can be found in the last chapters of *Conv* IV, arising out of the problem of nobility in the individual soul. It is an account of the ages of man, which approaches humanity from the opposite point of view to that adopted in *Inf*, by cataloguing the *virtues* proper to each age: *Adolescence* up to 25, *Youth* 25–45, *Old Age* 45–70, *Senility* after 70. Aeneas, as portrayed by Virgil, is taken as a pattern of the many virtues appropriate to the age which Dante had reached when he made his descent into Hell. This area of *Conv* owes much to Aristotle's *Ethics* and Cicero's *De Officiis*, the two sources most influential in giving Dante the idea for the general scheme expounded in *Inf* XI. The psychological interest displayed in *Conv* IV 24–9, taken together with the moral pessimism of the *canzoni*, and the fascination of the *Aeneid* go far towards explaining how the idea of *Inf* could take shape in Dante's mind. At this point in *Conv*, Dante is turning his attention to the varieties of human psychology in a way which foreshadows *Inf*.

The sheer complexity of the map of Hell, the physical geography and the corresponding moral classification, is apt to force the reader of *Inf* to give all his attention to taking his bearings. But the map is not the whole story. Against the pattern made by the classification of sins is set a more elusive pattern of reflection and comment, in which Dante is expressing, in a less systematic way, his view of his own situation and the fruits of his experience of life. The classification of sins itself is, of course, to some extent an expression of Dante's own moral preferences. He despises the fraudulent wolves more than the violent lions. But, when it comes to the characters who embody the sins, his condemnation is not necessarily proportional to their position in Hell and, indeed, is often strikingly discordant with it. There is a much stronger impression of dislike for Filippo Argenti, whom Dante meets in canto VIII in the circle of the angry and whom he would gladly have kicked back into the mud, than for many spirits further down, whom he treats with positive respect. Filippo Argenti was an ostentatious and overbearing political conservative in Florence, whom Dante probably opposed and disliked personally. He expresses a personal hatred separate from the moral classification. Though the moral classification is a serious statement of a view of morality and the punishments are made to fit the crimes with laborious ingenuity, many of the characters are made to talk about things unconnected with the sins which they represent. In this respect Dante treats his own classification cavalierly, and often seems to use it merely as an excuse to insert characters with whom he wishes to have converse for unconnected reasons.

The fact that Dante took such immense pains to set the *Comedy* firmly at Easter 1300 indicates that that date had a profound meaning for him. Apart from the fact that it was a centenary year, in which the pope announced special indulgences, the year 1300 probably had a dual significance. In the words of the first line of the *Comedy*, it was 'the middle of the way' for him, the year when he reached the age of 35, and, secondly, Easter 1300 was the period when his fatal involvement in the factional feud at Florence began. He may, we can imagine, have seen himself as entering at that point on a course of education in human wickedness analogous to his journey through Hell. Political experience looms very large in *Inf*, and the most obvious subsidiary pattern in the work is a line of reflection on politics, which runs through the *cantica* like a line of coloured thread in embroidery.

In a sense the most direct contact between Dante's own life and the subject matter of *Inf* is provided by the fact that he was himself on earth a condemned man. He had been exiled from Florence for the crime of barratry, that is, political corruption. The place of torment for shades guilty of this sin occupies a fairly prominent place in the eighth circle. In canto XXI Dante and Virgil come upon a lake of pitch, in which the barrators are being tortured by black devils with pitchforks. Two things are noticeable about this area of Hell: that it is pervaded by an air of rather grim humour and burlesque, which is unusual in *Inf* generally; and that it conveys a sense of the uncertainty of the exercise of justice. When Dante and Virgil appear, a devil is receiving a recent arrival from Lucca. He cries out that everyone in Lucca is a barrator except Bonturo Dati, who, the fourteenth-century commentators assure us, was famous for being by far the most corrupt man in the city. While Virgil goes forward to parley with the devils, from whom they require assistance to pass on to the next stage of their journey, Dante hides behind a rock and runs out only when he is called to stick close by his guide. The devils, who have absurd names, probably intended to be comic, eventually provide an escort round the lake. One of the spirits they see in the lake, an obscure personage of the generation before Dante's, guilty or not of barratry, had been murdered by another spirit whom we are to meet further down in Hell among the traitors. The march along the lakeside is broken by a quarrel between two of the demons, who in fighting fall into the lake themselves. It emerges later that the devils have misled the travellers about the road ahead of them: the devils are liars. This whole section conveys a sense of ironic unreliability about the tormentors and the punishments. An informed reader would have

recognised the appropriateness for the victim of a plainly
trumped-up charge of corruption of treating that particular
crime with a light touch, strengthened by the introduction of an
unusually cowering Dante who clearly expects the devils to
attack him.

But, in other sections, the commentary on Florentine politics,
specifically of the period 1300 to 1304, more generally the whole
Florentine political tradition, is in deadly earnest. It is the glutton Ciacco who supplies the first prophecy about Dante's
political future in canto VI. He foretells in veiled form the
conflict of parties leading to the Black Guelf *coup d'état* in 1301.
The dominant figure among the heretics in canto X, Farinata
degli Uberti, can be placed in that circle because he was commonly thought to believe in the mortality of the soul, but that
'magnanimous' or 'great-souled' spirit – the virtue is one that
Dante particularly admired – is significant for Dante chiefly
because of the role which he played in Florentine politics in the
heroic conflicts of Guelf and Ghibelline in the mid-thirteenth
century. After the Ghibelline victory at Montaperti in 1260,
Farinata, who was their leader, prevented the other cities from
razing Florence to the ground. Dante admires him as the
supreme example of the politician who put country before party.
In the end the Guelfs won and the Uberti were still in exile in
1300. He appropriately foretells that Dante, a Guelf by ancestry –
and perhaps in his own view a man who put country before party
like Farinata – will be exiled shortly. After Farinata, the most
prominent Florentine among the characters of *Inf* is Brunetto
Latini in the circle of the sodomists in canto XV. Brunetto, who
died in 1294, was a Florentine man of affairs and a vulgariser of
classical rhetoric and philosophy. His *Trésor* contained a brief
account of the conventional legend that Florence was founded
by a mixed population of Romans and people from the nearby
hill town of Fiesole. Brunetto foretells that the 'ungrateful,
malignant' Fiesolan strain in the Florentine population,
'avaricious, envious and proud' (the characteristics which Ciacco
had already attributed to Florentines in general), will drive Dante
out of the city.

Among the sodomists are also Tegghiaio Aldobrandi and
Jacopo Rusticucci, Florentines who were both active in the same
period as Farinata, but on the other side, as Guelfs. They were

remembered for having advised against the Guelf expedition of
1260 which led to the disaster of Montaperti, and were, therefore, peacemakers, and Dante greets them with affection as men
whose good reputation was well known to him. The meeting and
their questions give the fictional Dante himself an opportunity to
bewail the state of Florence. 'The new people and the quick
profits have generated pride and excess' (*Inf* XVI 73–4). Further
down in Hell are spirits whom Dante, in contrast, can identify as
his enemies, and condemn. It is Vanni Fucci, a man who was
famous among his contemporaries for committing a sacrilegious
theft from a church in Pistoia and who confesses his own 'bestial
life', who carries on the political story in canto XXIV. He tells
Dante of the coming defeat of the Whites outside Florence in
1302 and he tells it with relish because he was a leader of the
Pistoian Blacks: 'I have said this because it ought to grieve you.'
The worst Florentines, perhaps, appear far down among the
traitors in canto XXXII, where Bocca degli Abati, who betrayed
the Guelfs at Montaperti, is suffering and Carlino de Pazzi, who
was to betray the White exiles in 1302, is said to be awaited.
Dante's main point about his own political experience and about
Florentine politics, however, is the calamitous prevalence of faction and the virtue of those who can rise above it.

Inf is on the whole not the place to look for philosophy: Dante
is concerned here with a different aspect of humanity. There are
passages, however, which can be interpreted as expressions of
philosophical and religious points of view. The plainest of these
is in the section dealing with the circle of the heretics. The inhabitants of this circle are not, as one might expect, the perpe-
trators of the great heresies of the early Church, or the radical
religious rebels of the Middle Ages. They are, in fact, the free-
thinkers of thirteenth-century Italy who denied the immortality
of the soul, 'with Epicurus [admired for his rationalism in *Conv*
but now credited with more vulgar 'Epicureanism'] and all his
followers who made the soul die with the body' (*Inf* X 14–15),
and to emphasise their fault they suffer by being trapped in a
kind of graveyard, each in an open tomb. Besides Farinata, the
chief character is Cavalcante Cavalcanti, father of Dante's
friend, Guido. As they enter the city of Dis, which contains these
'Epicureans', Dante is assailed by the Furies who threaten that
Medusa the Gorgon will turn him to stone. Virgil makes Dante

shut his eyes, 'for if the Gorgon should show herself and you see her there would never be any returning above', and Dante, in an unusual kind of comment on the action of the poem, adds;

O voi ch'avete li 'ntelletti sani,
mirate la dottrina che s'asconde
sotto 'l velame de li versi strani.

O you who have sane intellects
take note of the teaching which is hidden
under the veil of the strange verses.

(*Inf* IX 60–63)

The dark meaning at which Dante hinted here was probably the danger of the destruction of the intellect by the false doctrine of the mortality of the soul, with which Dante felt he had himself once been threatened. When they meet Cavalcanti, he first asks why Guido is not with Dante. There is a double reference here to Guido's imminent death, less than five months later, and to Dante's close friendship with him. Dante replies in a famous enigmatic phrase: 'He [Virgil], who waits there, leads me through this place, perhaps [to her] whom your Guido held in disdain.' (*Inf* X 62–3) The reference is probably to Beatrice. Guido was reputed by his contemporaries to be an 'Epicurean' and, as we have seen, there is some evidence for it in his poetry. Whatever the true explanation of 'Guido's disdain', it is probable that Dante's purpose in the circle of the heretics was to dissociate himself from the materialistic free-thinking which was prevalent in some circles in Italy and with which he had flirted in his youth, by avoiding contamination by the 'epicurean' spirits and distancing himself from Guido.

The other area, in which we can look most fruitfully for attitudes extending beyond the ostensible subject-matter of *Inf*, is that part of the eighth circle occupied by the fraudulent counsellors. There are two great spirits in this region. One, Ulysses, is well known. The other, Guido da Montefeltro, was a prominent mercenary captain of the late thirteenth century. Ulysses, a Greek, is in this place because of his evil counsel in recommending the deception of the Trojan horse, which led to the defeat of the Trojans, the ancestors of the imperial Romans. Guido, a Latin, is there because he gave Boniface VIII the advice which led to the destruction of Palestrina, the fortress of the Colonna cardinals who were resisting Boniface, and, therefore, promoted the diversion of the Church from its proper path to the pursuit of war against fellow Christians. There is a parallelism in that they have offended against the two great terrestrial institutions, Empire and Church. The speeches which they make to Dante give them a different significance and a different parallelism.

For Ulysses, Dante invented a fate quite different from the one set out for him in the Odyssey. Dante's Ulysses did not return to Ithaca, but after leaving Circe embarked on a voyage of discovery into the Atlantic beyond the pillars of Hercules. Not even love of his family

> vince potero dentro a me l'ardore
> ch'i' ebbi a divenir del mondo esperto
> e de li vizi umani e del valore;

> could conquer the longing within me
> which I had to gain knowledge of the world
> and of human vices and human worth.

As he entered the unknown world of the Atlantic, he challenged his crew:

> Considerate la vostra semenza:
> fatti non foste a viver come bruti,
> ma per seguir virtute e canoscenza.

> Consider your birth:
> You were not made to live like brutes
> But to follow virtue and knowledge.

> (*Inf* XXVI 97–120)

They sailed into the Atlantic for five months and came in sight of a dark mountain, but their ship was destroyed by a whirlwind before they could reach it. The mountain, which they sighted but could not reach, was, we may assume, the base of the Earthly Paradise, to be attained by Dante much later after the painful ascent of Purgatory. The familiar Ulysses has been transformed into a symbol of the excessively aspiring human spirit. The Earthly Paradise is not attainable by man's unaided search. Ulysses is a noble pagan, but his quest, though directed towards virtue and knowledge, is misguided.

Guido's mistake, in contrast, is specifically Christian. He had

earned Dante's applause in *Conv* for becoming a friar at the end
of a lifetime of successful generalship. The rumour on which
Dante based canto XXVII was that he had been called out of his
holy retirement to give the pope military advice about Palestrina.
When he hesitated, the pope promised him absolution based on
the power to bind and loose, to absolve men from sins, which he
had inherited as the successor of St Peter. Guido gave in, only to
discover, too late, that even St. Francis, the founder of the order
which he had joined, could not save him from Hell. Guido's
story embodies an exaggerated reliance on ecclesiastical authority
which is parallel to Ulysses' reliance on humanity. Both are de-
ceived. Do these stories echo Dante's personal regrets? In the case
of Guido there is no reason to think so, except in the sense that
Dante may have become more disillusioned about the papacy as a
result of his political experience. Ulysses is more difficult. His
sentiments are both grander – his speech is perhaps the finest
sustained passage in *Inf* – and vaguer. Dante was a wanderer
who had sacrificed family to politics. Perhaps he felt that he had
pursued 'virtue and knowledge' on the purely human plane when
he should have attended to religious or moral duties.

The passages mentioned here may give some idea of the
temper of thought at some of the more striking moments in *Inf;*
they can give no sense of the vast, populated landscape or of the
poetry. *Inf*, like *VN*, *Conv* and *DVE* before it, explores an area
of interest, a group of inspirations, which for a while engaged
Dante's attention closely. The subject-matter of *Inf* is rather
more difficult to define than that of the previous books. It is, of
course, in the words of the letter to Can Grande – which actually
apply better to *Inf* and *Purg* than to *Para*, parts of which the
letter accompanied – 'the state of souls after death' and 'man
according as by his merits or demerits in the exercise of his free
will he is deserving of reward or punishment by justice'. But this
abstract description misses not only the poetic conception of *Inf*
but also the continual infusion of intense personal reflection. The
verdict of traditional popularity is on the whole right in judging
Inf to be Dante's most splendidly realised integration of life and
thought with art, and it is, therefore, perhaps the least easily
analysable. Like each of his main earlier works, however, it is
concerned to a large extent with completely new subject-matter,
evidence of an astonishing capacity in Dante to embark on

wholly new intellectual and artistic experiences and to create
something highly original in each one. His works are not only
entirely different: each one is so novel as to be unclassifiable in
terms of earlier literature. In none of these cases is it possible to
explain Dante's achievement as an extension, even the most far-
reaching extension, of an existing genre. Dante's breakthroughs
were made by establishing unexpected links, bringing together
the most diverse elements to create totally unexpected new compounds. *VN* is made by the amalgamation of the saint's life with
erotic poetry; *Inf* by peopling Virgil's underworld with the
household names of thirteenth-century Italy.

Dante's poetic style was no doubt changing throughout his
life. In *Inf,* however, the reader can see it in its mature splendour. It is hazardous to attempt to characterise it, because much
of its success depends on the constantly superb felicity in the
choice of words, often unexpected words, which English readers
find in Shakespeare and which can only be usefully analysed in
great detail and at great length. One of its more specific accomplishments is the sharp delineation of character, which has
been emphasised in this chapter as an intellectual as well as an
artistic innovation. Another power which Dante exhibits in a
very high degree is the capacity to express abstract ideas elegantly
within a strict metrical form. The further elaboration of this
technique is perhaps the most obvious stylistic development after
Inf. It is very prominent in the more philosophical passages of
Para. In comparison with his earlier verse, the poetry of the
Comedy is more stately; it nearly always maintains a convincing
mood of high seriousness. But readers of the *Comedy* probably
remember it above all for the continual vividness with which
Dante evokes specific scenes either in metaphor or simile or in
direct description. It may be Farinata degli Uberti explaining
how the bitterness of the battle of Montaperti beside the Arbia
made him for ever hated by the Guelfs of Florence:

> lo strazio e 'l grande scempio
> che fece l'Arbia colorata in rosso.

> The anguish and the great slaughter
> that made Arbia coloured red.   (*Inf* X 85–6)

Or it may be the figure of Brunetto Latini fleeing from the fumes
in Hell recalling the runners in the annual race at Verona:

Poi si rivolse, e parve di coloro
che corrono a Verona il drappo verde
per la campagna; e parve di costoro
quelli che vince, non colui che perde.

Then he turned away, fleeing like one of those
who run for the green cloth at Verona
over the country; and he seemed like one
who wins, not one who loses.

(*Inf* XV 121-4)

Or it may be the description of Dante and Virgil reaching the
shore below Purgatory in the early morning, like lonely travellers
coming to any remote beach at dawn:

L'alba vinceva l'ora mattutina
che fuggia innanzi, sì che di lontano
conobbi il tremolar de la marina.

Dawn was conquering the morning hour
which fled before it, so that from afar
I recognised the shimmering of the sea.

(*Purg* I 115-17)

By this vividness Dante not only makes the other world live, but
also adds sharpness and pathos to the fate of his characters and
satisfies the most romantic expectations of his readers, without
ever compromising the gravity of his theme. This book is about
Dante's ideas rather than his poetic achievements, but it is as well
to remember that, especially in the greatest passages, for instance
the canto of Ulysses, the abstract meaning is not completely de-
tachable from the poetry.

Henry VII, evangelical religion and Monarchy

The writer of *Conv* and *Inf* was to suffer another upheaval of ideas caused by political events.

The history of Italy between 1309 and 1313 was dominated by the meteoric rise and fall of a new political force in the peninsula, the Emperor Henry VII. Henry, Count of Luxembourg, young, ambitious and attractive, was elected king of the Romans in 1308. He quickly made it plain that he intended to take the Italian opportunities offered by his office much more seriously than his immediate predecessors, that he meant to go without delay to Italy, to establish an imperial peace and to be crowned emperor at Rome. His ambitions were favoured by the policy of Pope Clement V, exiled in France, and the papacy gave him moderate encouragement, sanctioning the coexistence of an imperial power in return for Henry's promise to respect the integrity of papal possessions. He was at first surprisingly successful. He established control over most of Lombardy in 1311 and moved South. His chief enemies in Italy were Guelf Florence and King Robert of Naples, but the power which turned the scales against him was that of King Philip IV of France, who was alarmed by the possibility of a Rhineland prince becoming a real power in Italy. He forced the pope to change his policy and to side with the Guelf allies of France, Florence and Naples. Nevertheless, Henry was crowned at Rome in 1312. His fortunes were in serious decline but the future was still not clear, when his death of malaria in 1313 shattered the hopes of his supporters.

In distant retrospect, this attempt by a German princeling to revive the imperial power may appear simply quixotic. To many contemporary Italians, however, it was a new political inspiration. The imperialist cause was revived not just for Henry's brief reign but for a generation. Nobody embraced the cause more fervently than Dante, but his enthusiasm, though certainly strengthened by his personal interest in Ghibelline success, was not just the eccentric idealism of a political exile. Imperialism had powerful political interests behind it and seemed to many other people to offer the best hope in a world of political fragmentation and endless conflict. The new turn of Italian politics forced Dante to confront the great medieval problem of temporal and spiritual power.

We are slightly better informed about Dante's political life in the period 1310 to 1314 than in the previous years of exile, because he composed a small number of 'political letters' – in reality manifestos written in splendid rhetorical Latin and intended for publication. In October 1310, on the eve of Henry's invasion, Dante wrote to the princes and peoples of Italy exhorting them to welcome the new political dawn. He set out a traditional view that the Empire and the papacy were dual and equal powers governing respectively the temporal and spiritual aspects of life on earth, as shown by providential history. The Italians, in particular, should welcome the Roman Emperor. Dante made it clear that he assumed, as he was justified in doing at that point, that the pope recognised Henry. In the spring of the following year, with Henry's star in the ascendant, he wrote a letter addressed to the Florentines and containing his bitterest denunciation of them. At this point Dante must have hoped and expected that the establishment of an imperial peace in Italy would bring his own personal revenge against his Guelf enemies in Florence. He also wrote to Henry, placing his mission firmly in the line of Aeneas and Caesar and urging him to march directly against the centre of the evil in Florence.

These writings reveal Dante as an exultant supporter of Henry. His Ghibelline theory of imperialism, first expressed academically in *Conv* IV, has become a political doctrine held now with eager anticipation of its imminent fulfilment. His next and last political letter, however, was written several years later in the disappointment which followed Henry's failure, and is concerned not with the Empire but with the papacy. Pope Clement V died in 1314. He had abandoned his moderate support of the Ghibellines and at the end of his life he was committed to their enemies, Robert of Naples, Florence and the king of France. After nine years in France the papacy had become largely French, as well as Guelf. Early in the vacancy following Clement's death, Dante addressed a letter to the remaining Italian cardinals. It is essentially a plea for the return of the papacy to Rome which has been betrayed like Jerusalem. The Church has been driven out of its course, and the cardinals cultivate canon law instead of theology. Their duty is to rescue the papacy from the Gascons and return it to Rome.

The letters show us two stages in Dante's political evolution: imperialism, expecting papal support, in 1310–11 and extreme disillusionment about the papacy in 1314. The imperialism, though strengthened, was not new. In the end, the main effect of the experience of Henry's reign, in which Dante evidently participated with intense emotion, was to turn him into a bitter critic of the Avignon papacy. A new theme of evangelical denunciation of the modern papacy and all its works, not found in the writings which we have described in earlier chapters – except for part of *Inf* XIX, which is probably a late addition – now becomes prominent, especially in the two books composed in the period *circa* 1308–14, *Purg* and *De Monarchia* (Monarchy). The political logic of this development is quite clear. Many other Ghibellines became bitter enemies of the Avignon papacy for the same reason. But in Dante the political change was accompanied by a new intensity of religious feeling which was less common. He became not merely a political critic of the papacy, but a religious radical, embracing apparently for the first time an apostolic view of the Church, which became a burning conviction.

There is no evidence about the sources of Dante's religious radicalism, but it is such a powerful motif that we are driven to speculate about its origin. The transformation of Beatrice from love object into saint in the *VN* led us to invoke religious movements as a likely influence on Dante's imagination. It seems probably that we should look to related aspects of Italian religious life for some of the conceptions expressed in *Purg* and *Mon.* The two striking novelties which we shall find in those books are, firstly, the idea of a Church committed to complete apostolic poverty and, secondly, the idea that the contemporary Church was going through a process of apocalyptic degradation from which it would be rescued by a saviour. Neither of these ideas is very uncommon, but both were strikingly prominent in Dante's day among the rigorists in the Franciscan Order, of whom there were many in central Italy. These 'spiritual' Franciscans wished to follow a strict rule of poverty, but were opposed, and sometimes persecuted, by the majority in their order and by ecclesiastical authority in general. They reacted by embracing radical views about the Church as a whole. They were numerous and prominent in the Franciscan homeland of central Italy. Dante's reference in *Para* to one of the leading contemporary 'spiritual' writers, Ubertino da Casale, and to Joachim of Fiore, whose ideas were adopted by some of the spirituals, shows his familiarity with them. It would, in any case, have been impossible for him to avoid knowing about them: they were too prominent in Tuscan and Umbrian life. Dante's political quarrel with papal authority probably opened his mind to the influence of religious ideas which were easily available but would not otherwise have been attractive to him. This may seem a bare and mechanical hypothesis to explain an immense inner revolution, but most of the story of that upheaval is completely lost. We can only sketchily imagine its character.

Mon is the most difficult of Dante's works to place chronologically. The view adopted here is that it was written in the period of the collapse of the imperialist venture, towards the end of Henry's life or shortly after, *circa* 1312–14. But the reader must be warned that this is a hypothetical view with which some scholars would disagree. *Mon* is divided into three books, which approach the subject-matter from three quite distinct points of view. Book I is a philosophical argument for the necessity of a single world monarchy; Book II is a historical demonstration that the Roman Empire is destined to fill that role; Book III is a primarily theological demolition of the arguments in favour of ecclesiastical property and jurisdiction.

Dante had put a philosophical case for world monarchy briefly in *Conv* IV 4. In *Mon* I he elaborates this argument. The way in which he does it is strongly reminiscent of the philosophical atmosphere of *Conv*, although the two arguments have different purposes. In *Conv* Dante wanted to mark out a separate sphere of political authority for the Empire, so that the sphere of philosophy, with which he was principally concerned, should not be infringed. In *Mon*, the purpose of the argument, to separate lay from spiritual authority, is quite different. The purpose of politics, Dante now argues, is to advance humanity towards its ultimate end. Since the specific purpose of man, as distinct from other parts of the created universe, is 'the state of apprehending by means of the possible intellect' (*Mon* I iii), the aim of political life must be to help men to exploit this intellectual potential.

This must be done by the whole human race together, and for this work peace is above all essential. Dante argued that peace could best be secured by a single all-powerful monarch.

Many of the arguments which Dante adduces in favour of world monarchy are essentially based on an analogy between society and the whole of creation. The world is ruled by a monarchical God who is the prime mover; mankind is, therefore, better ruled by a single monarch. Unity is, in all things, better than multiplicity. Dante here expresses a conflation, characteristic of his philosophy, of the Aristotelian prime mover and the neoplatonic source of goodness. He also develops two more particular arguments about justice and about free will, in which themes appear that are important in his other late works, particularly *Para.* Justice (*Mon* I 12) in the ruler is maximised if his will is pure and his power total, the latter prerequisite obviously to be found in a world monarch. The great obstacle to the purity of the will is cupidity, which is minimised in a world ruler because he has by definition nothing to gain and, therefore, no temptation to act for base motives like ordinary monarchs. Free will (*Mon* I 12) is the exercise of rational judgement unimpeded by appetite, and is man's distinctive faculty and God's greatest gift to him. Bad political systems – following an argument derived ultimately from Aristotle – enslave men's wills and prevent them from being truly human. Only a world monarchy can be disinterested and, therefore, allow the free exercise of the will.

In Dante's day, the philosophical theory of the State, that is to say the adaptation of ideas taken from Aristotle's *Ethics* and *Politics* to medieval Christian uses, had not had many practitioners. The principal theories available were those of Aquinas, who had made a very influential attempt to incorporate Aristotelian concepts into a hierarchy of values, culminating in divine law, that is, Christian revelation. For Aquinas, the purpose of human States was to create the framework within which a Christian life could be lived, and human law was an application, within the limits of human reason, of divine law. To this extent the State and its promotion of earthly well-being was, as Aristotle had argued, good and necessary. Dante owes much to this tradition, and he could hardly have conceived of his own theory unless he had known something about the Thomist theory. The use which he made of Aristotle, however, was very different.

Firstly, Dante showed little or no interest in the internal constitution of States. His is essentially a theory about world monarchy, in a sense international politics, an approach which
stemmed from his Ghibelline interest in a supreme imperial
power. Secondly, he made a radical departure from Thomist
theory in postulating a dualism which set up a separate terrestrial
purpose for the State: the promotion of man's intellectual faculties. Although it allows a proper sphere for lay politics, Thomist theory was designed to show how it should be subordinated
to an ultimate religious purpose. Dante, on the contrary, gave the
State a separate, non-religious purpose. In thus using Aristotle to
construct a philosophical justification for a separate lay authority, not subordinated to ecclesiastical or religious ends, Dante
was highly original, indeed revolutionary. The medieval world
had seen many defences of lay power against papal interference,
but a philosophical theory of the self-sufficient secular State was
a novelty. In the sphere of philosophical ideas Dante's political
theory is his most original creation, though because it was tied to
the Roman Empire, it was destined to have little permanent
influence.

In his theory of the actualisation of human intellectual potential, Dante referred, in an obscure passage, to Averroes' commentary on Aristotle's *De Anima* to support his view that the
intellectual activity of all men was necessary to this process. This
reference laid him open to the charge, which helped ecclesiastical
critics to get *Mon* burned after his death, that he held a heretical
view on one of the central issues in the dispute between Averroists and their opponents. Averroes thought that the possible
intellect in man was a temporary offshoot of the universal intellect, which was reunited with the whole after a man's death.
Dante, in fact, explicitly rejected this view in *Purg* XXV, putting
into the mouth of Statius, the Roman poet who accompanied
him at this stage of the *Comedy,* the authoritative words

> this is that point
> that made one wiser than you err,
> so that by his teaching he separated
> the possible intellect from the soul

> (*Purg* XXV 62–6)

Whether the 'one wiser than you' was Aristotle or Averroes,

Dante was certainly here stating an orthodox position that the separate soul remained separate after death. It is conceivable, of course, that he put this into *Purg* to correct the impression given by *Mon*. In any case, what he wrote in *Mon* is unlikely to have been intentionally heretical. It may have meant simply that many minds were necessary to realise human potentialities. The passage does, however, show that he was juggling with Aristotelian ideas in a novel way, to produce a secularised theory of the State, and that he was basing it on the highly favourable view of man's rational intellect which he had displayed in *Conv*.

The argument of *Mon* II is essentially an expanded version of the defence of the Roman Empire in *Conv* IV. He once thought, he tells us, that the Romans conquered the world by force of arms; now he recognises that divine providence was at work. The method of *Mon* II is to treat the events of Roman history, drawn from Virgil, Livy, Augustine and other authors, as evidence of the hand of God in history, in much the same way as the events of the Old Testament. Properly understood, Dante argues, the events of secular history can be interpreted as expressions of God's will. The noble actions of the Roman heroes, the miraculous events which favoured Rome's advancement and the success of the Romans in superseding the earlier empires of Assyria, Egypt, Persia and Macedonia were all evidence that the Romans were intended to rule the world. The Roman Empire was established in time to undertake the crucifixion of Jesus by the authority of all mankind, so that his atonement could be made effective for all men. Dante drew his examples and ideas from a number of sources. The strongest influences on his general conceptions were probably Virgil and Orosius, the fifth-century Christian historian; Virgil, because of Anchises' speech to Aeneas foretelling Rome's imperial destiny; Orosius, because he provided the theory of Rome's unique and essential function in making Christianity possible.

Mon I and II could be regarded without much distortion as expansions of views already stated in *Conv*. The argument of *Mon* III is new, and deals with a sphere of thought in which Dante had not previously shown interest. Pope Clement V claimed the right to instruct Henry VII about his temporal duties in Italy. This claim was based on theories about papal authority which had been built up over the preceding century and which depended primarily on canon law, that is to say on papal decrees and on the interpretation of them by ecclesiastical lawyers. These are the 'decretalists' whom Dante names as his adversaries. His purpose in *Mon* III is to destroy their structure of thought and to replace it by his own theory of the Church. He states at the beginning, as the basis of his argument, the premise that the only valid evidence about the nature of the Church is to be found in the Bible. No later 'tradition' has any independent validity, so that the question essentially turns, for Dante, on the interpretation of biblical texts. Much canonist theory also depended on the use of the Bible, so there was a large area in which he was prepared to dispute with them.

Dante accepts the exegetical system of drawing mystical significance out of passages of scripture. He objects not to the method in general but to the particular interpretations urged by canonists. One of the texts most commonly used to support the idea that the spiritual power was superior to the temporal was the story of the creation of the sun and the moon in Genesis I 16. The sun was taken to stand for spiritual power and the moon for temporal. The moon took its light from the sun, so the temporal power was similarly dependent. Dante argued that the sun and the moon could not be given this significance, chiefly on the ground that God created them before he created man. Since temporal and spiritual powers were in the Aristotelian sense 'accidents' of humanity – qualities added to humanity not essential to its existence – God would not have intended to prefigure them with parts of the creation prior to man. Moreover, as a fact of astronomy, the moon, Dante thought, had an independent motion and could not be regarded as dependent on the sun. With similarly ingenious arguments Dante dismisses all his selection of texts commonly cited by the canonists.

He then turned his attention to some non-biblical arguments, of which the most important was the case based on the Donation of Constantine, the famous document, forged in the eighth century, which purported to record the grant of imperial power to the pope by the Emperor Constantine. Dante did not question the authenticity of the Donation – it appears in several places in the *Comedy* as one of the tragic events of world history – but he argued that the reason why it was invalid was because it offended against the essential character of both the Empire and the

Church. No emperor could give away a part of imperial authority because the Empire was divinely ordained to be a total world power. Conversely, the Church could not by its nature receive property or jurisdiction, except as an intermediary receiving alms for the poor, because Jesus forbade it: 'Provide neither gold nor silver nor brass . . .'. Dante's own positive view of the nature of the Church, which he went on to express in the final chapters of *Mon* III, was simple. The Church was the apostolic body established by Christ and ordered by him to live in poverty and humility. It could not be treated like the State, fitted into an Aristotelian order of nature. It was simply founded by God, as the New Testament recorded, and could not be defined in any other way. In Aristotelian terms the 'form' of the Church, that which defined its nature, was the life of Christ.

Because of man's peculiar position in the hierarchy of being, suspended between spirit and matter, possessing an incorruptible soul and a corruptible body, he had two ends and must aim at two distinct 'beatitudes': the beatitude of this world, dependent on the intellectual and moral virtues, and the beatitude of the other, dependent on the theological virtues of faith, hope and charity. One is entirely under the jurisdiction of the emperor, the other entirely under the jurisdiction of the pope. This uncompromising dualism was Dante's answer to the problem posed by the catastrophic overlapping of temporal and spiritual powers which destroyed the enterprise of Henry VII, as the polemical tone of Book III shows. Dante says it is directed against enemies of truth who are the pope, the haters of the principate and the decretalists (*Mon* III 3). Like Dante's other original creations, it is produced by an unusual convergence of ideas, in this case, however, not fused by poetry but clearly divided between the three books: the philosophical idea of man's rational nature, the mission of Rome and the apostolic Church. The dualism also represents two layers of his own thought. It seems likely that before this period Dante had taken little interest in theology or ecclesiology. Faced with the political situation of *circa* 1313 he seems to have refurbished philosophical and historical arguments which he had formulated some years earlier and added to them the new and much more urgent theological message of Book III. The almost exclusive enthusiasm for the potentialities of human reason which dominated *Conv* paradoxically made it easier for him to construct a quite separate argument for an entirely spiritual, mendicant Church when the need arose.

Purgatorio *and the return of Beatrice*

The plan of *Purg* is in outline much simpler than that of *Inf*. Dante and Virgil emerge from the earth on the shore at the foot of the mount of Purgatory. After altercation with Cato, who guards the entry to purgatory, they set off to climb the steep mountain. Purgatory proper starts some distance up the mountain and they do not reach it until canto IX. Up to that point they meet the shades of people who made the essential repentance only at the moment of death, and of a large group of politically prominent 'negligent rulers' still awaiting the time to enter Purgatory, which extends through cantos IX–XXVII. The path of the travellers winds round the mountain in seven stages, in each of which the shades are labouring appropriately to expiate one of the seven capital sins. Though he does not suffer the penalties of the spirits in Purgatory, Dante participates in this expiation and when he has passed through the purifying fire he is in some sense freed of sin. On the way up he has acquired a second companion, the Latin poet Statius, who has gained entry to Purgatory – this is Dante's invention – by a secret conversion. Dante, Virgil and Statius emerge before the Earthly Paradise, situated on a plateau at the top of the mountain, which is shown to them by a lady called Matelda. Then a fantastic mystical procession appears (canto XXIX), bringing with it Beatrice (XXX), on whose appearance Virgil disappears. Dante makes a confession to Beatrice and is taken through the river of Lethe to be cleansed of the memory of sin. He then sees the mystical procession transformed into a pageant representing the history of the Church, and Beatrice makes a prophecy about the coming of a mysterious saviour. Finally, he is taken through the river Eunoe which restores to him the memory of good.

By far the most enigmatic part of *Purg* is the central figure of Beatrice, who reappears here in person for the first time since her death in *VN*. The difficulty of interpretation is the same: the combination of a real person, a dazzling poetic creation and a religious symbol. Beatrice reappears with ambiguous hints of biblical significance similar to those in *VN* where she was – in some way – like Christ, preceded by Cavalcanti's Giovanna as John the

Baptist. Here her appearance on the stage is heralded by similar references to texts: such as the bride from Lebanon of the Song of Songs, usually held to refer to the Church as the spouse of Christ, and the cry 'Blessed is he who comes', which greeted Christ on Palm Sunday. She now has the attributes of her position as a redeemed soul in heaven: judgement and knowledge. Her first function is to recall to Dante's mind the memory of his sins and to compel him to a humiliating and painful confession, whilst her second role is to explain things which his mortal understanding would not grasp. But there is no way to penetrate into the experience – religious, emotional, poetic – which made Dante turn back in about 1312 to the Beatrice of 1290. He must have felt himself called back to the religious idealism which inspired *VN*, but we cannot go beyond this. An allegorical interpretation, in which Beatrice signifies grace or theology, contains some truth, but is one-sided. She does not seem to be a literal Beatrice plus an allegorical grace, like the ladies of the philosophical *canzoni*; she is a more integrated complex of meaning. Much of the rest of *Purg* can be interpreted in more or less straightforward language. Beatrice is not susceptible to the same kind of treatment.

Purgatory itself, omitting the Ante-Purgatory below and the Earthly Paradise above, resembles Hell in being a hierarchy of sins with strictly appropriate punishments. In all other aspects it is very unlike Hell. It is directed by angels, not demons, and the spirits in it are working towards their eventual release. It has none of the sprawling squalor of Hell. Entry to it is like going into a controlled ecclesiastical environment, and the rapid progress of Dante through it is like a Church service. It has a liturgical atmosphere; the sins of pride, envy, anger, accidie or sloth, avarice, gluttony and lust are being purged systematically by a regular procedure, like the repentance and absolution in a mass. In the cornice devoted to each sin, there are representations of opposed virtues, beginning in each case with an example from the life of the Virgin Mary followed by at least one pagan, classical example. Thus on the cornice of pride there are carvings of the Annunciation and of a legend of the Emperor Trajan consoling a widow, both indicating humility. In all but one of the cornices there are references to the singing of appropriate parts of church services: in the cornice of pride, for example, the shades,

bent under heavy burdens which it is their punishment to carry,
are saying the Lord's prayer. Dante is not, as he is in Hell, merely
an observer. Though he does not suffer the torments of the sin-
ful, the weight of his sins is lifted from him as he moves up the
mountain and emerges from the final purifying fire with his will
'free, upright and healthy' (*Purg* XXVII 140). Hell is a tour
conducted by Virgil; Purgatory is a purification from which
Dante emerges changed and able to understand what he had not
understood before.

Within the framework of Purgatory and the Earthly Paradise
there are two converging themes, both of which reach their
climax in the utterances of Beatrice. One is Dante's own life, the
other is the Church.

The meeting with Beatrice initially takes the form of a confession. She greets him with a reminder of his unworthiness,

> How did you think yourself worthy to climb the mountain?
> Did you not know that man here is happy?
>
> (*Purg* XXX 74–5)

and then forces him to admit that he had turned aside from the
right path after her death distracted by 'The present things with
their false pleasure' (*Purg* XXXI 34–5). Beatrice's references to
'a young girl or other vanity' suggests that the ordinary sins of
the flesh are an important part of what Dante has to repent.
Dante also refers to his own sins as he climbs up the mount of
Purgatory in a way which suggests that his confession to Beatrice
is a genuine acknowledgement of neglect of her and attachment
to other women. Among the gluttons, he meets his old friend
Forese Donati, who died in 1295, raised up in the short space of
five years to an unexpectedly high level of Purgatory by the
prayers of his devout wife. Dante associates himself with Forese's
sins: 'If you recall to mind what you and I were together, the
present memory will still be painful' (*Purg* XXIII 115–7).
Further down, the fictional Dante also confesses his particular
fear of punishment for the sin of pride, and it must be in recognition of his own weakness that the famous speech in that circle
is about the vanity of fleeting artistic glory: the fame of Cimabue
has given way to that of Giotto, who will be superseded too.
When Forese's companion among the gluttons, the poet Bon-
agiunta, compliments Dante as the creator of the *dolce stil*

nuovo, readers are presumably intended to remember the transitory fame of Giotto, the greatest living painter.

Although Dante goes to Beatrice as an ordinary penitent, the rejection of his past intellectual and literary errors is more clearly presented in *Purg* than the expiation of his ordinary sins. Presumably the two were closely connected in his mind. The line of doctrinal self-correction begins in Ante-Purgatory (*Purg* II), when Dante meets a Florentine musician, Casella, who entrances him, and Virgil too, by singing *Amor che ne la mente mi ragiona,* the second of the allegorical love poems expounded in *Conv.* Cato recalls them abruptly from that distraction to the serious business of climbing the mountain. Dante could not have chosen that poem unless he had meant to expose both the literal love of the flesh and the allegorical love of the spirit which it expressed. Some way up the mountain (*Purg* XVIII) Dante calls on Virgil to expound the nature of love, and he begins by giving a philosophical description of the process of love. An image is presented to the mind, which, if it is beautiful, arouses the appetite of the sensitive soul to desire. Yes, says Dante, but how do we choose between good and bad? The explanation of that, Virgil replies, goes beyond my capacity into the sphere of faith, and you must, therefore, ask Beatrice to explain. The choice of the object of love is governed by reason and by free will.

This is one of several places in *Purg* where Dante emphasises, as in the case of this analysis of love, the inadequacy of pagan reason; Plato and Aristotle could not understand how God worked. Therefore Statius, the Latin poet fictionally converted to Christianity for the purpose of this poem, not Virgil, is given the task of explaining the nature and origin of the soul to Dante in canto XXV. The speech is not included here to record any changes in Dante's view about the philosophical theory of the soul – the doctrine which Statius gives on this difficult matter is not essentially different from what Dante had written in *Conv* IV – but to make a point about the relationship between philosophy and theology. The immortality of the unified soul, including the intellect, is an essential Christian truth. Even after death, the soul can suffer in Purgatory for its sins. 'One wiser than you' (Aristotle or Averroes) misunderstood this, and only a Christian can explain it properly.

Elsewhere in *Purg,* Dante also seems to be concerned to reject once again the courtly love conception of love as an irrational, uncontrollable passion. Just before he enters the last purifying fire at the top of Purgatory, he hears his illustrious precursor, the Provençal poet Arnaut Daniel, described in *DVE* as a great poet of love and clearly regarded by Dante as one of the founts of his poetic tradition, disclaim his 'past folly' in the language of the troubadours, the original language of courtly love. In canto XVIII Dante makes Virgil assert the role of rational choice in love.

There is a resemblance between this double rejection of philosophical materialism – especially the mortality of the soul – and irrational eroticism in *Purg* and the earlier rejection of the same things in *VN*. In a sense Dante is recoiling again from the same psychological and philosophical temptations, turning a second time to Beatrice, for similar reasons. But he now has behind him not only the Cavalcantian love poetry, but also the spiritualised philosophy of love contained in the poems and prose of *Conv*. The rediscovery of Beatrice is similar to his original recognition of her, but is now raised dialectically on to a more complex level.

Her arrival is also associated with the extraordinary spectacle of the mystical procession. The vision which Dante sees across the stream in the Earthly Paradise is a collection of biblical and ecclesiastical symbols grouped around a griffon, whose double-nature, half lion and half eagle, symbolises Christ's humanity and divinity, drawing a chariot, representing the Church. The symbols are those of the gifts of the holy spirit, the virtues and the books of the Bible. After his confession to Beatrice and cleansing in the water of Lethe, Dante sleeps. He is awakened to be shown the procession transformed into a pageant of the history of the Church. The chariot, representing the Church, is first attacked by an eagle (the Empire's persecution of the early church), then by a fox (the early heresies), and again by the eagle, which leaves its feathers on the chariot (the Donation of Constantine). It is cloven by a dragon (Mohammedanism), it puts forth seven heads (sins?), a harlot appears seated on it (the papal court) kissing a giant (the French court), who drags chariot and harlot into a wood (the captivity of the Church in France). This is an adaptation of the imagery of the Book of Revelation to actual history, which is foreshadowed in Dante's writings only by *Inf* XIX. That part of *Inf* was probably added after the death of

Clement V in 1314. The adaptation of the imagery of the Apocalypse to specific events of contemporary politics was characteristic of radical thought in the Franciscan Order, and may well show influence from that quarter, though the more general moral use of the same material was common in medieval writing and preaching. It seems to be a new element, however, in Dante's thought.

The picture of modern corruption, presented graphically by the pageant in canto XXXII, is the culmination of prominent passages earlier in *Purg.* One of the characters met in Ante-Purgatory is Sordello, like Virgil a poet of Mantua, unlike the Augustan poet a citizen of modern Italy, a land neglected by the Emperor and strife-ridden. Dante used him as a pretext for bewailing the unruly politics of the Italians, their rejection of the effective rule of Roman law and the German Emperor's neglect of Italy. In canto XVI the theme is taken up by an unidentified character called Marco Lombardo. Dante asks him why the world is so destitute of virtue, and he replies first that the fault is in men, not in their stars. Lack of good law and obedience to existing law has allowed the social world to go astray. The particular ill he complains of is the confusion of spiritual power with temporal:

> Soleva Roma, che 'l buon mondo feo,
> due soli aver, che l'una e l'altra strada
> facean vedere, e del mondo e di Deo.

> Rome which made the good world used to have
> Two suns, by which one road and the other
> were shown, that of the world and of God.

(Purg XVI 106–8)

This is the doctrine of *Mon* III, that the two lights of Church and Empire are equal. In modern Italy the proper division has been confused by the papal assumption of temporal power in competition with the Empire. The circle of the avaricious is dominated by the figure of Hugh Capet, founder of the French dynasty to which Dante's contemporary Philip IV belonged. His main function is to condemn the avarice of the kings of his line during Dante's lifetime, ending with a prophecy of events after 1300. He foresees Charles of Valois winning Florence by treachery in 1301, and then the humiliation of the Pope Boniface VIII at Anagni in 1303. Boniface, who had been criticised as a simoniac in *Inf* XIX, is here Christ's vicar, re-enacting Calvary:

> Veggiolo un'altra volta esser deriso;
> veggio rinovellar l'aceto e 'l fiele,
> e tra vivi ladroni esser anciso.
> Veggio il novo Pilato ...
>
> I see him a second time mocked
> I see the vinegar and gall renewed
> And him slain between living thieves
> I see the new Pilate ...
>
> (*Purg* XX 88–91)

Philip IV of France is also the giant of the pageant in canto XXXII, who defiles and captures the papacy. The view of contemporary history presented in *Purg* is that Italy, torn by strife, has been betrayed by neglectful emperors and grasping popes and that the papacy has been degraded by the French. There is no specific reference to Henry VII, but the view of the degradation of the papacy expressed here is specifically related to the Avignon papacy and probably to the last years of Clement V. The man who wrote *Mon* III was inspired by the same convictions as the man who wrote *Purg*: he believed that the proper order was a division of power between a terrestrial empire and a spiritual papacy, each wholly and exclusively competent in its own sphere.

Near the end of *Mon* Dante wrote:

Ineffable providence has set two ends for men to strive towards: the beatitude of this life, which consists in the operation of his own virtue and is figured in the Earthly Paradise, and the beatitude of eternal life, which consists in the enjoyment of the vision of God, to which man's own virtue cannot ascend unless assisted by divine light, which is to be understood by the Heavenly Paradise ... We come to the first by the teaching of philosophy, if we follow it by exercising the moral and intellectual virtues; to the second by spiritual teaching, which transcends human reason, if we follow it by exercising the theological virtues, faith, hope and charity. (*Mon* III xv)

The last cantos of *Purg* can be regarded as a poetic rendering of this philosophy. When he left Purgatory, Dante could see the Earthly Paradise across the River Lethe. He could not enter it until his renewal, by confession to Beatrice, had been followed by immersion in Lethe, which restored his innocence, but its character was partially explained to him before that by the lady, mysteriously called Matelda, whom he saw gathering flowers on the other side of the river. The Earthly Paradise is a delightful creation of bucolic fantasy, but it also has a serious philosophical purpose. Matelda explains that it corresponds not only to the biblical Eden, but also to the golden age imagined by the classical poets. It is recalled in some lines of Virgil, which Dante adapted for incorporation in his poem as follows:

> the age is renewed,
> justice returns and the first time of man
> and a new progeny descends from heaven.
>
> (*Purg* XXII 70–2)

Earthly beatitude was 'figured' by the Earthly Paradise, not merely because it was a place of blessed innocence, but because it embodied to perfection the virtues accessible to man without Christian revelation. Below, in Ante-Purgatory, Dante had seen four stars 'never before seen except by the first people', and then at night three different stars. The mystical procession included groups of four and three nymphs, representing the four cardinal virtues (temperance, prudence, fortitude and justice) and the three theological virtues (faith, hope and charity). The four say, 'we are nymphs here and in the sky we are stars'. It seems probable that Dante intended the first four stars to represent the pagan or philosophical equivalents to the four cardinal virtues which can be stars or nymphs. The 'first people', who saw the four stars, were Adam and Eve. Dante thus connects both pagan and Christian ideas of innocence with those human virtues which can be practised without the aid of Christian revelation.

Dante's own approach to the Earthly Paradise in canto XXVII was preceded by a dream in which he saw Leah and Rachel, traditionally symbols of the active and contemplative lives, foreshadowing the perfection of those accomplishments which he was to see in Matelda. The Earthly Paradise was a place in which the active and intellectual virtues were practised. In this sense it 'figured' the perfection of rational earthly life described in *Conv* and *Mon* I, in contrast to the spiritual perfection made available by Christ and the Church, 'figured' by the mystical procession and Beatrice. The two great poetic creations of the last cantos of *Purg,* the Earthly Paradise and the mystical procession, thus correspond to the two ways of earthly and spiritual beatitude which Dante identified theoretically at the end of *Mon*. They show the same almost incongruous contrast: the Aristotelian humanism of the earthly kingdom set against the biblical austerity of the spiritual church; the soft poetic beauty of the Earthly Paradise against the evangelical ferocity of the apocalyptic pageant. *Purg* represents a stage when Dante's imagination is preoccupied by this dualism of the old philosophical values, which he still accepts, and the second dimension of his new religious enthusiasm.

5 Paradise

In *Paradiso* Dante and Beatrice rise up through the concentric heavens, conceived very much as they had been in *Conv.* The landscapes of *Inf* and *Purg* were imaginary, but much of *Para* takes place in the real world as it was depicted by medieval cosmologists. The structure of the heavens, described in the course of the journey, is not a fiction but, on the contrary, is itself an essential part of the truth which Dante intended to convey in *Para.* The stages of ascent are also used for the unfolding of a course of doctrine which is imparted to Dante by Beatrice and other inhabitants of heaven. It is arranged in an intellectual hierarchy corresponding to the levels of the heavens, partly because Dante's understanding grows in power as he draws nearer to the source of truth. He begins with questions of physics and ethics, fairly accessible to reason, and ends with the truths of theology, comprehended as they cannot be on earth. The hierarchy of knowledge is not a gratuitous arrangement: it is essential to Dante's metaphysics that proximity to God higher up in the heavens should confer a different quality of understanding. Dante adopted the dramatic device of introducing characters into each of the circles – mostly famous people like the Emperor Justinian or St Thomas Aquinas – who are redeemed souls, normally resident in heaven, but come down, like Beatrice, into the circles of planets and stars to enlighten him about appropriate subjects. The matching of speakers to subjects is plainer than in *Inf* and *Purg*: we meet more obvious authorities, like the Emperor Justinian for imperialism and St. John for theology. There is one large exception to this general plan: Dante's dialogue with his ancestor Cacciaguida, in cantos XV–XVII. Apart from that, *Para* is, from one point of view, a didactic work, following a pattern of systematic revelation of rising levels in understanding. The use of the heavenly circles and the concentration on rational exposition recall the educational enterprise left half-finished in *Conv.* A crude outline of the plan is as follows:

Circle	Chief characters	Main topics
Empyrean XXX–XXXIII	St. Bernard	Heaven
Crystalline heaven XXVIII–XXX	Beatrice	Angels
Starry heaven XXIII–XXVII	St. Peter, James, John	Theological virtues
Saturn XXI–XXII	Peter Damian St. Benedict	Contemplative life
Jupiter XVIII–XX	The Eagle	Justice
Mars XIV–XVIII	Cacciaguida	Dante's life
Sun X–XIV	St. Thomas Aquinas Bonaventure	Mendicant orders, creation, wisdom
Venus VIII–IX	Charles Martel	Influence of stars
Mercury V–VII	Justinian	Roman Empire
Moon II–V	Piccarda	Moon shadows Free will

Dante's universe remained to the end neoplatonic. His new ecclesiastical enthusiasms seem to have had no impact on that part of his thought. The idea of divine power, emanating from the Empyrean and transmitted through the hierarchy to all parts of creation, which he sketched sometimes rather obliquely in *Conv,* became in *Para* a vision embracing the circles of planets and stars and heaven itself. It is expressed poetically by the ascent of the spirits of Dante and Beatrice, drawn irresistibly towards the object of their desire by the irradiation of light, which fills their world with increasing brightness, and by the expansion of joy with growing understanding. This is not metaphor; it is a description of the facts, the expression of his belief that the universe is actually held together by the three forces of light, reason and love, which are in a sense identical. When they enter the Empyrean, at the end of their journey, Beatrice tells him that it is made of light, reason and love:

> pura luce:
> luce intellettüal, piena d'amore;
> amor di vero ben, pien di letizia.

> pure light;
> intellectual light full of love,
> love of true good full of happiness.

> (*Para* XXX 39–41)

The Empyrean is heaven, the unmoving centre of the universe, though in another sense it surrounds the outermost circle of the heavens. As Dante and Beatrice pass out of the created universe through the Chrystalline heaven they move from circles apparently centred physically on earth to circles centred on God. The physical world gives way to a non-physical world in which virtue has replaced time and space as the dominant organising principle. The Empyrean is shown to Dante by St. Bernard, the great mystical theologian of the twelfth century, presumably thought by Dante to have approached as closely to the understanding of God as any mortal man could. It is full of light. He is allowed to look at the Godhead and sees, though he cannot describe it, the source of 'the love that moves the sun and the other stars'. The Godhead is both Aristotelian prime mover, the source of all physical motion in the universe, and source of love.

As they entered the Chrystalline heaven, Dante had looked up to see a point of intense light. Beatrice explained: 'from that point hang the heavens and all nature' (*Para* XXVIII 41–2), and that it is the focal point of all time and space. He also sees the nine orders of angels in circles around the point of light. Angels, in *Para* as in *Conv*, are pure intellects, uncorrupted by matter. Some of them are the movers of the heavenly spheres and play an important part in the transmission of divine influences to the lower levels of creation. Dante seems to have accepted the idea that the creation of man was planned by God to make up for the loss of the fallen angels, now in Hell, by the subsequent reception of redeemed souls in heaven.

The principles of the universe are stated in the first lines of *Para*:

> La gloria di colui che tutto move
> per l'universo penetra, e risplende
> in una parte più e meno altrove.

> The glory of him who moves everything
> penetrates through the universe and glows again
> more in one part and less in another.

Dante himself glossed these lines in his letter to Can Grande. He explains there the main sources of his cosmology: God is conceived as prime mover in the Aristotelian sense, the ultimate origin of all influences; these influences are transmitted by the intermediary intelligences or angels in the neoplatonic manner. 'The lower intelligences have their effect as it were from a radiating body, and, after the fashion of mirrors, reflect the rays of the higher to the one below them.' The exposition of the cosmological-metaphysical theme is continued in one of Dante's remarkable virtuoso demonstrations of his art of philosophical poetry in canto II, where he discusses the technical question of the dark patches on the moon. The fictional Dante here, in the circle of the moon, propounds to Beatrice the theory, which he had stated in *Conv*, that the dark patches are caused by variations in the density of the moon, leading to variations in the reflection of light. Beatrice corrects this, saying that the variations are not of density but of the character of the substance itself. A principle is at stake: that the heavenly bodies vary in essential character, in 'virtue'. This is important, because it accounts for the differentiation of the unified divine power in the lower parts of the created universe. The unified influence which emanates from the Chrystalline heaven is split up among the stars of the Starry heaven and is passed on to the circles below. The circles 'take from above and act on what is below' (*Para* II 123). Each of the heavenly bodies takes its character from the 'blessed movers', the angels which control it. Beatrice in this passage is made to correct Dante's earlier scientific opinion, but the effect of the correction is to strengthen the consistency of the neoplatonic cosmology.

Later on, in the circle of Mercury, Beatrice explains that God creates human souls directly as he once created the angels, the heavens and primal matter; they are therefore incorruptible, except by the effects of sin. Other things, however, are created by the 'radiation and movement of the sacred lights', that is, the stars (*Para* VII 141), which are intermediaries between God and other parts of creation. The theme is taken up again in the circle of the Sun, where Dante puts into the mouth of the spirit of Aquinas a speech with which the real Aquinas would not have been entirely sympathetic. The phenomenon to be explained is the variability of human nature. Aquinas says that everything created is indeed the reflection of the 'idea' in God: His power is directed to the nine orders of angels, and from them it descends to all parts of the universe, bringing men and other beings into existence. Both the matter, on which the celestial influences act, and the celestial influences themselves are variable, and therefore men, being compounds of spirit and matter, are not uniform. Dante continued to hold a theory of the universe which was conventional in being a combination of Aristotelian physics, neoplatonism and Christianity, but tended rather to emphasise the neoplatonic element. The metaphysical passages in the circles of the Moon, Mercury and the Sun, quoted in the last two paragraphs, emphasise that the creating and controlling power of God is mediated through the heavenly circles before it reaches man and the earth.

Apart from cosmology, the philosophical issue most prominently raised below the circle of Saturn is free will. The occasion for it is the appearance in the circle of the Moon of a girl whom Dante had known on earth, Piccarda, sister of his friend Forese and his enemy Corso Donati. After taking religious vows, she was dragged out of the convent by her brothers and forced into a political marriage. Though she submitted unwillingly, it is still a defect in her that she had broken her vow. Dante is troubled by the apparent injustice of this. Beatrice explains that the application of violence does not destroy the inner freedom of the absolute will, which need not be affected by coercion, and goes on to instruct Dante about dispensation from vows. In the making of a vow, she distinguishes between the decision to sacrifice, which can never be erased if free will is to be properly exercised, and the content of the sacrifice, which may be changed by ecclesiastical dispensation. This argument is worked out on the borderline between human reason and divine authority. Parts of it are drawn from Aquinas, but the fictional Dante admits his inability to arrive at these conclusions unaided.

> Io veggio ben che già mai non si sazia
> nostro intelletto, se 'l ver non lo illustra
> di fuor dal qual nessun vero si spazia.

> I see well that there can be no satisfaction
> of our intellect unless illuminated by that truth
> beyond which no truth ranges.

> (*Para* IV 124–6)

Dante wins Beatrice's approval: he is beginning to understand, through approximation to the 'eternal light', though there are vestiges of his earlier misunderstanding of it. The changing of vows, so far as it is allowed, is entirely subject to ecclesiastical authority:

> Ma non trasmuti carco a la sua spalla
> per suo arbitrio alcun, zanza la volta
> e de la chiave bianca e de la gialla.

> But let no one change the load on his shoulder
> by his own will without the turning
> of both the white and the yellow key.

> (*Para* V 55–7)

This is a very different angle on the free will question from that of the argument of *Mon* I. The emphasis is now on inner freedom and on the religious and ecclesiastical aspects, whereas it had previously been on the impossibility of free will under political constraint.

It is possible to see a parallel – in the sense that they are corrections of views stated in *Mon* – between this treatment of free will and the treatment of justice, another topic which had been considered politically in *Mon* I. As Dante and Beatrice enter the circle of Jupiter, they see a cloud of lights, which forms itself first into the opening words of the Book of Wisdom, 'Love justice you who judge the earth', then into the outline of an eagle, symbolising Roman justice. The lights in the eagle are the spirits of just kings: David, Hezekiah and Constantine are mentioned. They speak with a single voice, which offers help to Dante with the baffling problem of the good pagan, condemned, through no fault of his own, for his lack of Christianity. The truth about divine justice in such matters, they tell him, is utterly beyond earthly comprehension: only God knows who will ultimately be saved. This inscrutability is driven home by the identification of some of the redeemed souls making up the eagle, who include, apart from the obvious just kings, two totally unexpected spirits. One is the emperor Trajan, posthumously saved in medieval legend, the other an obscure Trojan leader Rhipeo, chosen for this honour by Dante only because Virgil applied the epithet 'most just' to him in the *Aeneid*. As the Eagle tells Dante, using a scholastic term of art:

You do as one to whom the thing by name
is known; but its *quiddity*
you cannot see unless another disclosed it.

(*Para* XX 91–3)

The message of this circle is that ultimate, divine justice seems arbitrary to men familiar only with earthly justice.

In both the passages just mentioned Dante has deliberately dwarfed human conceptions by setting them against the awful inscrutability of the divine mind. He is not necessarily condemning what he had written about free will and justice in *Mon*, but is correcting it by setting it against another huge dimension. The dimension of divine truth is in a sense the subject of *Para*. In the lower circles much emphasis is placed on the apparent hard irrationalities of Christian doctrine. In Justinian's account of the providential history of Rome, in the circle of Mercury, he includes the destruction of Jerusalem by Titus, 'the vengeance for the vengeance for the old sin' (VI 92–3), the revenge against the Jews for their execution of the atonement. Beatrice takes this up in the next canto, to explain to Dante's questioning mind why God ordered Christ's atonement. The reason for this method of redemption, Dante admits, is beyond his understanding. Before she goes on to explain the necessity of Christ's sacrifice, Beatrice tells Dante:

This decree, brother, is buried
from the eyes of anyone whose understanding
has not been completed within the flame of love.

(VII 58–60)

Regarded in this light, *Para* falls into two sections, separated by the ascent through the circle of Saturn in canto XXII. Up to that point, the matters expounded to Dante are either comprehensible to mortals exercising reason or they are beyond Dante's mortal understanding, and consequently the emphasis on the inscrutability of God increases up to the circle of Jupiter. After ascending the Jacob's ladder of contemplation in the circle of Saturn, Dante's intelligence is transformed, so that it is capable of understanding theological truths.

The main figures in the circle of Saturn are Peter Damian, an eleventh-century monk who was made a cardinal against his will,

and St Benedict, founder of the Benedictine Order and author of
the Rule, which was the basic document of medieval mon-
asticism. They are chosen as spokesmen for the Christian contemplative life, with the implication that it is by the pursuit of
that life that a man can acquire understanding of theological
truths. After passing through that circle, Dante can already see
the hosts of the redeemed spirits beyond the created universe. His
mind and his eyes have acquired a higher power. Beatrice can say
at last 'Open your eyes and look at what I am': he can now
endure her smile, which lower down in the heavens would have
blinded him at its full power. The rest of *Para* is concerned with
theology and heaven.

Does the emphasis on the inadequacy of human reason, which
runs through *Para*, mean that Dante had abandoned some of the
convictions of *Conv* and *Mon* I? The message of *Para* is to some
extent ambiguous. In the circle of the Sun there are two rings of
lights, each containing twelve spirits of wisdom, presided over by
Aquinas and Bonaventure, the greatest doctors of the Dominican
and Franciscan orders. Most of the spirits are impeccable Christian teachers like Bede and Anselm, yet very surprisingly one of
them is Siger of Brabant, the most famous Averroist thinker in
late thirteenth-century Paris. Dante, who says here that Siger 'syl-
logised invidious truths', cannot have been unaware of the general significance of his teaching, at least of the fact that he was
denounced by Aquinas, in a famous dispute, because of his attachment to non-Christian interpretations of Aristotle. The next
canto, a few lines on, begins:

> O insensata cura de' mortali,
> quanto son difettivi silogismi
> quei che ti fanno in basso batter l'ali.

> O senseless care of mortals,
> how defective are the syllogisms
> which make you beat your wings down.

(XI 1–3)

Though he thinks syllogisms have a limited value, Dante must in
the passage on Siger be recognising some virtue in the kind of
philosophical enquiry for which Siger was notorious. Later, in
canto XXVI, when he is interrogated by St John about love,
Dante is called upon to say from what authorities he has learned

about the love of God. The three he cites are Aristotle, the Old Testament and the Book of Revelation. Aristotle taught him that the whole universe turns towards God in love. The answer is approved by St. John:

> Per intelletto umano
> e per autoritadi a lui concorde
> d'i tuoi amori a Dio guarda il sovrano.

> by human intellect
> and by authorities concordant with it,
> keep the chief of your loves for God.

(XXVI 46–8)

It seems that Dante continued to regard reason as an important source of truth, even about divine things. The last quotation is consistent with the passages in *Conv* which give reason the power to carry the mind some distance towards truth until the point where the guidance of the Holy Spirit is required. The difference between *Conv* and *Para* is that Dante's main subject-matter here is precisely the kind of truth which is never fully accessible to reason.

Dante remained passionately concerned with the relationship between Empire and Church, which plays almost as large a part in *Para* as it does in *Purg*. The appearance in the circle of Mercury of the Emperor Justinian to speak for those who pursued the life of honour and fame is really an excuse for another rehearsal of the providential history of Rome. As one of the great Christian emperors and also the organiser of the compilations from which medieval lawyers drew their knowledge of Roman law, Justinian was a suitable exponent of the theme. He tells very briefly the story of republican and imperial Rome, and then carries it on through the Middle Ages so that Charles II of Naples and the other Guelfs of Dante's own day can be placed in the long line of futile opponents of the Empire. Finally, when they reach the Empyrean, Beatrice points out the seat in the Celestial Rose of heaven awaiting 'the high Henry [Henry VII] who to direct Italy shall come before she is ready for it' (XXX 137–8), and prophesies that the treacherous Clement will be thrust down into Hell. Dante also maintained with similar vehemence his attachment to the idea of an apostolic church. Constantine is among the just kings in the eagle in the circle of Jupiter, but his Donation is condemned:

> Now he knows how the evil deduced
> from his good deed is not harmful to him
> though the world was destroyed by it.

(XX 58–60)

The most powerful passage about the contemporary Church in the whole *Comedy* is in canto XXVII, where St. Peter himself denounces his successors, specifically Boniface VIII:

> He who usurps on earth my place,
> my place, my place which is vacant
> in the presence of the Son of God
> has made of my burial-ground a sewer
> of blood and filth . . .

(XXVII 22–5)

At the sound of this denunciation Beatrice blushes, and Dante compares her blush to the eclipse of the sun at the time of the crucifixion. Peter predicts that providence will act again as it did when Scipio saved Rome by defeating Hannibal.

Dante's ecclesiastical interests are illustrated by a new topic which is given a prominent place in *Para,* the great contemporary question of the mendicant orders. Throughout Dante's lifetime, the Franciscan and Dominican orders were the most vital institutions in the Church in Italy and the dispute between rigorists and moderates, among the Franciscans in particular, was a great public issue. In cantos XI–XII, Aquinas and Bonaventure describe the origins of the two orders, lamenting that few now keep to the ideals of Dominic and Francis. Dante puts into the mouth of Bonaventure a rejection of both extremes in the Franciscan order. All this is moderate and conventional opinion, but the picture is complicated by the fact that Dante includes, among the twenty-four luminaries in this circle of the Sun, the apocalyptic writer Joachim of Fiore, whose works inspired the subversive and heretical views of the extreme radical Franciscans. Joachim's presence is an anomaly parallel to that of Siger, who is placed symmetrically in the same position in the other circle of twelve. We must suppose that, although Dante did not in general agree with the radical Franciscans, he is indicating that he believed there was an important role for apocalyptic prophecy of the kind which he himself had expressed in the climax of *Purg*.

It is largely due to *Para* that, after being condemned as an enemy of the Church in the decade after his death because of *Mon*, Dante came later to be regarded as an orthodox catholic writer. How much had his views actually changed since he wrote *Mon*? It is made clear that on the proper roles of papacy and empire they had not changed at all. He was still an imperialist, condemning the Donation of Constantine as a world-historical catastrophe, which implies that he was in agreement with most of what he had written in *Mon* II and III. But *Para* has nothing to say about the philosophical justification for the separate lay state in *Mon* I or about the two beatitudes of terrestrial and celestial life, postulated at the end of *Mon* III. It has been maintained that the subordination of reason to revelation in *Para* is incompatible with the two beatitudes based on philosophy and theology. The subordination in *Para*, however, is related to theological questions: it is not clear that Dante intended to exclude an independent sphere for reason in earthly and philosophical matters. A clear-cut answer about the relationship of *Mon* and *Para* is impossible because Dante did not go over the same philosophical ground. Though he did not repent of *Mon* as a political programme, the Earthly Paradise of secular wisdom must have lost its positive attraction. What had happened was probably a change in his focus of interest, rather than a change of opinion. The new focus was a vision of heaven, in which theological truth was what mattered.

But in the first place *Para* was a vision of heaven, not an account of theology. Dante several times indicates that he considered his last work to be not a story, an allegory or a treatise, but a vision. 'The human intellect in this life', he says, commenting on the early lines of *Para* in the letter to Can Grande,

when in exaltation, reaches such a height of exaltation that after its return to itself memory fails, since it has transcended the range of human faculty. And this is conveyed to us by the Apostle where he says, addressing the Corinthians: 'I know a man (whether in the body or out of the body, I cannot tell; God knoweth) how that he was caught up to the third heaven, and heard unspeakable words, which it is not lawful for a man to utter.' ... This again is conveyed to us in Matthew ... And in Ezekiel ... And should these not satisfy the cavillers, let them read Richard of St. Victor in his book *On Contemplation*; let them read Bernard in his book *On Consideration*; let them read Augustine in his book *On the Capacity of the Soul* . . . But if on account of the sinfulness of the speaker they should cry out against his claim to have reached such a height of exaltation, let them read Daniel, where they will find that even Nebuchadnezzar by divine permission beheld certain things as a warning to sinners and straightway forgot them.

At the beginning and the end of *Para*, Dante bewails his feeble power to remember or express, not what he wished to say, but what he had *seen*. Not only that, he believed also that he was intended, on divine authority, to convey the vision to his fellow men on earth. Several times in the later parts of the *Comedy* he is told that he must go back and tell what he had seen: by Beatrice after she has commented on the mystical pageant:

> as they are presented by me
> so do you signify these words to the living
> in the life that is a race to death.

> (*Purg* XXXIII 52–4)

and by St. Peter after he had conveyed a similar message about the Church and its fate.

The vision and its significance are inseparable from Dante's view of the contemporary Church and from the political situation in which he found himself in his last years, when *Para* was being written. The Ghibelline cause did not by any means die with Henry VII. A new German king, elected in 1314, took up the anti-Guelf banner, and although he played little part in Italy in Dante's lifetime, the imperialist party there was active. A brief spectacular revival of Ghibellinism in Tuscany in 1315 led to Dante being condemned still more fiercely at Florence, this time to public execution if he were captured. When an amnesty was offered a year later, it was too late for him to accept the humiliation of compromise, as he might well have done a decade earlier. 'Can I not everywhere behold the sun and the stars?' he wrote in a letter to Florence: the politics of the city had lost their immediacy for a man whose imagination was filled with visions of the Empire, the Church triumphant and the heavens. The cockpit of Guelf–Ghilbelline conflict was now eastern Lombardy. Ghibelline lords and cities were there engaged in a series of wars of increasing bitterness with Pope John XXII, a new and very aggressive leader of the Guelf alliance in Italy, which was to extend far beyond Dante's death. These courts were the refuges of his last years. Almost nothing is known of his life at this time beyond the names of two protectors: Can Grande della Scala, tyrant of Verona, the recipient of the letter about the *Comedy,* and Guido Novello da Polenta of Ravenna. They are enough to place him in the context of active imperialist politics. His last (unidentified) illness began in 1321 when he was on an embassy from Ravenna to Venice.

Dante's most extended commentary on his own life is in his exchange with his remote ancestor Cacciaguida in the circle of Mars. After reflecting at length on the corruption of modern Florentine society, Cacciaguida foretells Dante's future as he saw it in 1300. His exile is already planned in Rome. It will be bitter: he will lose everything, learn 'how hard a path it is to go down and up another's stairs', be tormented by vicious companions. He will be befriended by the Della Scala family, whose greatness will appear even before Clement V's betrayal of Henry VII. The perspective in which Dante saw his own life had changed considerably since his reflections in the early years of exile woven into *Inf.* He now saw his exile, in a proud exaggeration of his own importance, plotted at Rome at Easter 1300, and his political life thereafter set in the framework of the imperial–papal conflict which now obsessed him, and in which he believed he had a destined role to play. After absorbing the forbidding prophecy, the fictional Dante asks what he should do about the record of his journey in the other world. Cacciaguida says he must tell it all, sparing no one: 'Make all your vision manifest and let them scratch where the scab is' (XVII 128–9). He has been told about the fate of the great in order that he should make it known.

Cacciaguida assured Dante, however, that he would live to see himself revenged on his enemies. This is only one indication that Dante to the end expected a favourable revolution in human affairs. There are predictions of that kind in all three *cantiche.* Unfortunately they defy interpretation beyond a certain point. At the beginning of *Inf,* when Dante is saved from the she-wolf signifying avarice by Virgil, he is told that she will be killed by a *veltro* – greyhound – who will be the salvation of Italy. No one has been able to explain who the *veltro* was to be. After the pageant, which showed the degradation of the Church in *Purg*, Beatrice says that the eagle, the Roman Empire, shall have a successor and that

> a five hundred, ten and five,
> sent by God, shall slay the thief
> with that giant who sins with her.

(XXXIII 43–5)

The numbers – 515, DXV – recall the numbers used in prophecies based on the Book of Revelation, which inspired Dante, but no one has identified the figure who is to destroy the corrupt papacy (the thief) and the French monarchy (the giant), and indeed Beatrice herself says that her words are 'obscure like Themis and Sphinx'. After St. Peter has condemned the modern Church in *Para*, he foretells that providence will bring succour to the world, as Scipio saved Rome. This salvation seems to be expected soon. The saviour whom Dante expected cannot be Henry VII, but the speeches of Beatrice and St Peter connect salvation with the Empire. Dante apparently continued to expect some form of imperial revival in Italy which would regenerate the Church and Italian politics. His political hopes were linked with the apocalyptic view of the Church which he had borrowed from the religious radicals. The pure apostolic church, preparing souls to join those whom he had seen in his visionary heaven, had, as its necessary counterpart, the earthly empire. His prophecies were dark, probably because he did not know who the saviour was to be, but he believed that it was his appointed mission to make the prophecy.

The visionary Dante of *Para* has travelled a long way from the philosophical commentator of *Conv*, even though he has retained many of his convictions. The adoption of the apostolic religion of *Mon* III is a great division between the early and the late periods of exile. The Dante of *Para* has also advanced beyond the Virgilian disciple of *Inf*. The elements in the poem connected with his final conception of himself as the prophetic declaimer of modern corruption and imperial salvation to come provide the strongest connecting links between the parts of the *Comedy*. It is probable that the vision belongs to a late stage in Dante's life, long after *Inf* was planned. But, in the *Comedy* as it stands finally, the idea that Dante's journey is a mission of high destiny is already present at the beginning. When Virgil proposes their descent into Hell, Dante protests that he has no claim to follow Aeneas, who had been chosen to be the father of Rome, and whose journey had been necessary to prepare both the Empire and the papacy. The only other man, supposed by medieval legend to have made such a journey, was St. Paul. 'I am not Aeneas, I am not Paul' (*Inf* II 32). Virgil encourages Dante on the ground that he comes to fetch him at the command of the Virgin, St Lucy and Beatrice. To those who tried to hinder their passage near the beginning Virgil said:

> Non impedir lo suo fatale andare:
> vuolsi così colà dove si puote
> ciò che si vuole, e più non dimandare.

> Impede not his fated going:
> it is willed there, where can be done
> that which is willed, and ask no more.

(*Inf* V 22–4)

By the end of his life Dante had placed himself in the line of Aeneas and Paul, among those who had a place in the providential history of Empire and Church.

Conclusion

Dante's final exaltation of his own role in history was the culmination of a lifetime of individualistic and self-conscious
exploration of art and thought. What general importance does
his work have? Two kinds of significance can be seen in his
works: on the one hand, the originality of some of his creations;
on the other, the capacity to give expression to the mind and
spirit of his age.

As a theorist, Dante's most original construction was the political thought of *Mon,* a powerful and novel defence of the independent validity of the secular state. It had comparatively little
influence in the long run, because the imperial power became
insignificant in Italy a generation after Dante's death. For
different reasons, his other works remained inimitable achievements. The *Comedy* was too vast, idiosyncratic and successful to
be the beginning of a new literary genre. In one sense, Dante was
a genius isolated by his originality. He was not a founder of
schools, except in the more limited field of poetic composition.

Dante is an essential figure in European civilisation because of
the special magnificence with which he expressed certain central
movements of the European mind. The vision of a hierarchical
universe, embracing matter and spirit, which the men of the high
Middle Ages accepted in one form or another, was never so
memorably expressed as in Dante's personal, neoplatonic version,
Para. In contrast, *Mon,* though doomed by its connection with
the Empire, was the earliest theoretical assertion of the self-
sufficiency of secular society. Because of his local background,
Dante's works are also strongly imprinted with characteristics
drawn from the world of the Italian city. This was very different
from the milieu which created scholastic philosophy. He wrote
with a strong sense of realistic individuality of character and for
an audience of lay readers of Italian. He drew on the intense
religious feeling of local Italian cults and on the mythology of
antiquity. Dante was both the greatest literary exponent of the
scholastic vision and the first great writer of Renaissance Italy. In
spite of his eccentricity and his self-absorption, he therefore ex-

presses imaginatively an incomparably wide conspectus of the early European mind.

There is one last thing to be said. Dante's originality is difficult to define because he was neither a great original philosopher – like, say, Aquinas or Descartes – nor an artist responsible for a massive single innovation, like his contemporary, the painter Giotto. He was a universal genius whose way of envisaging men and the world subtly transformed the whole European imagination. Approaching the *Comedy* from the thirteenth century, the time-traveller feels that he has come for the first time to a work which is spiritually akin to the world of Michelangelo and Shakespeare. This impression is not an illusion, but it is difficult to define satisfactorily. The most that can be said with confidence is that the fascination of classical antiquity and, more important, the vision of highly individual human destiny set against a Christian neoplatonic universe, which we have found in Dante, became characteristic of Renaissance Italy and Europe. This was a product of the meeting between the Italian city mentality and northern scholasticism. The first fruit of that encounter appeared in Dante's generation. The most obvious merit of the *Comedy* is that it contains more sustained poetic beauty than any poem written since; but it also contained a new way of looking at the world.

Further reading

Translations of Dante's works
English-speaking readers who have even a few words of Italian
will often find a bilingual edition the most useful.
The Divine Comedy. Bilingual edition with an up-to-date
Italian text and full notes by C. S. Singleton: *Inferno* (1970);
Purgatorio (1973); *Paradiso* (1975) (two volumes each).

The Temple Classics edition by H. Oelsner and P. H.
Wicksteed (three volumes, 1899–1901), with outdated Italian
text but good translation and notes, remains perhaps the most
convenient for the general reader.

The verse translation by D. L. Sayers (three volumes, Penguin, 1949–62) has good notes, but no Italian text.

Vita Nuova. Translation by B. Reynolds (Penguin, 1969).

Dante's Lyric Poetry. Bilingual edition with full notes by K.
Foster and P. Boyde (two volumes, Oxford, 1967).

Monarchy. Translated in *Monarchy and Three Political Letters*
by D. Nicholl and C. Hardie (London 1954).

Convivio. Translated by P. H. Wicksteed (Temple Classics,
1903).

De Vulgari Eloquentia. Translation by A. G. Ferrars Howell.

Letters. Text, translation and notes by P. Toynbee: *Dantis Alagherii Epistolae* (Oxford, 1966).

Books about Dante in English
*A Dictionary of Proper Names and Notable Matters in the
Works of Dante* by P. Toynbee, revised by C. S. Singleton
(Oxford, 1968), is an invaluable reference work.

There are innumerable books about Dante. The following is a
selection of fairly recent works in English, or translated into
English, all of which are particularly illuminating.

E. Auerbach, *Dante: Poet of the Secular World* (Chicago and
London, 1961).

P. Boyde, *Dante's Style in his Lyric Poetry* (Cambridge, 1971).

U. Cosmo, *Handbook to Dante Studies* (Oxford, 1950).

C. Till Davis, *Dante and the Idea of Rome* (Oxford, 1957).

K. Foster, *The Two Dantes* (London 1977).

E. Gilson, *Dante the Philosopher* (London, 1948), also published as *Dante and Philosophy* (New York, 1963).

R. Hollander, *Allegory in Dante's Commedia* (Princeton, 1969).

J. A. Mazzeo, *Medieval Cultural Tradition in Dante's Comedy* (Ithaca, 1968).

C. S. Singleton, *Dante Studies*: 1, *Commedia: Elements of Structure*; 2, *Journey to Beatrice* (Cambridge, Massachusetts, 1957 and 1967).

The works mentioned below provide background reading to the various aspects of Dante introduced in individual chapters.

Chapter 1

The most recent biography of Dante is G. Padoan, *Introduzione a Dante* (Florence, 1975). Readers will find there references to the meagre documents bearing on Dante's life and the problems raised by his biography, relating to this and later chapters.

The most interesting study of Dante's relationship to the tradition of courtly love is in the first two essays in B. Nardi, *Dante e la Cultura Medievale* (2nd ed., Bari, 1949). Most of the Italian poetry which influenced Dante, including all that survives of Cavalcanti's, is in Gianfranco Contini (ed.), *Poeti del Duecento* (two volumes, Milan and Naples, 1960).

The standard edition of the *Vita Nuova* is by Michele Barbi (Florence, 1932). There are several important editions of the shorter poems, including those in *Vita Nuova*, all containing notes which are worth consulting: Gianfranco Contini (ed.), *Dante Alighieri: Rime* (2nd ed., Turin, 1946), M. Barbi and Francesco Maggini (eds), *Rime della 'Vita Nuova' e della Giovinezza* (Florence, 1956), M. Barbi and V. Pernicone (eds), *Rime della Maturità e dell'Esilio* (Florence, 1969), K. Foster and P. Boyde (eds), *Dante's Lyric Poetry* (two volumes, Oxford, 1967). Among the recent interpretations of the *Vita Nuova* are C. S. Singleton, *An Essay on the Vita Nuova* (Cambridge, Massachusetts, 1949) and D. De Robertis, *Il Libro della Vita Nuova* (2nd ed., Florence, 1970). The hagiographical background has been partially explored by V. Branca in 'Poetica del rinnovamento e tradizione agiografica nella *Vita Nuova*' in *Studi in Onore di I. Siciliano* (vol. 1, Florence, 1966).

Chapter 2

For the complicated background of Florentine and Italian politics in this period, by far the best guide is R. Davidsohn, *Storia di Firenze* (Florence, 1956–65, translated from the German original, 1896–1925), volumes iii–iv.

The standard edition of *De Vulgari Eloquentia* is by A. Marigo (2nd ed., Florence, 1957). The fullest edition of *Convivio* is that by G. Busnelli and G. Vandelli (two volumes, 2nd ed., Florence, 1968), much criticised for exaggerating Dante's dependence on Aquinas. The best text, without explanatory notes, is now that by Maria Simonelli (Bologna, 1966). The best general account of Dante's philosophical evolution will be found in E. Gilson, *Dante et la Philosophie* (Paris, 1939), translated as *Dante the Philosopher* (London, 1948), reissued as *Dante and Philosophy* (New York, 1963). The most acute investigations of the origins of the ideas in *Convivio* are in some of the essays included in Bruno Nardi, *Saggi di Filosofia Dantesca* (2nd ed., Florence, 1967) and *Saggi di Filosofia Medievale* (Rome, 1960).

Chapter 3

Though there are many annotated editions of *The Divine Comedy*, there is no ideal one. The best text is G. Petrocchi's *Dante Alighieri: La Commedia Secondo l'Antica Vulgata* (four volumes, Milan, 1965–7), without explanatory notes. A good annotated edition is that by N. Sapegno (Florence, 1955–7).

On the general character of *The Divine Comedy*, the reader can only be referred to the works of a few leading critics, often expressing conflicting views: M. Barbi, *Problemi di Critica Dantesca* (two volumes, Florence, 1934–41), E. Auerbach, *Dante: Poet of the Secular World* (translation of German original of 1929, Chicago, 1961), C. S. Singleton, *Dante Studies*, I, *Commedia: Elements of Structure* (Cambridge, Massachusetts, 1954), B. Nardi, 'Sull'interpretazione allegorica e sulla struttura della "Commedia di Dante"' in *Saggi e Note di Critica Dantesca* (Milan and Naples, 1966). The letter to Can Grande is best read in *Dantis Alagherii Epistolae*, P. Toynbee (ed.), (2nd ed., Oxford, 1966). On its authenticity, a recent view (against) is stated by B. Nardi in *Il Punto sull'Epistola a Can Grande* (Florence, 1960). The plan of *Inferno* was well elucidated by Edward Moore in an essay in *Studies in Dante, second series* (Oxford, 1899).

Chapter 4
Italian reactions to Henry VII are fully set out in R. Davidsohn's
Storia di Firenze, vol. iv. A more recent account of his ex-
pedition is W. M. Bowsky, *Henry VII in Italy* (Lincoln,
Nebraska, 1960). Dante's political letters are in *Dantis Alagherii
Epistolae*. His attitude to the Roman Empire and its background
have been examined by C. Till Davis in *Dante and the Idea of
Rome* (Oxford, 1957).

The best annotated edition of *Monarchia* is that by G. Vinay
(Florence, 1950). Its text has been superseded by P. G. Ricci's
edition (Milan, 1965). The fullest examination of Dante's political thought is by F. Ercole, *Il Pensiero Politico di Dante* (two
volumes, Milan, 1927–8). There are good comments, demonstrat-
ing the irreconcilable differences between it and the Thomist
standpoint in E. Gilson's *Dante and Philosophy*, B. Nardi's *Saggi
di Filosofia Dantesca* and, especially, his *Dal Convivio alla Commedia* (Rome, 1960).

The background of religious radicalism can be approached
through D. L. Douie, *The Nature and Effect of the Heresy of
the Fraticelli* (Manchester, 1932). Much of the symbolism and
allegory of *Purgatorio* are well elucidated in C. S. Singleton,
Dante Studies, 2, Journey to Beatrice (Cambridge, Massachusetts, 1967).

Chapter 5
There are examinations of the philosophical and theological
teaching of *Paradiso* in the books cited earlier by E. Gilson and
B. Nardi and in J. A. Mazzeo's *Structure and Thought in the
Paradiso* (Ithaca, 1958) and *Medieval Cultural Tradition in
Dante's Comedy* (Ithaca, 1960). An interesting discussion of the
speculative question of Dante's messianism and sense of personal
mission is to be found in B. Nardi's 'Dante Profeta' in *Dante e la
Cultura Medievale*.

Index

Past Masters

AQUINAS Anthony Kenny

Anthony Kenny writes about Thomas Aquinas as a philosopher, for readers who may not share Aquinas's theological interests and beliefs. He begins with an account of Aquinas's life and works, and assesses his importance for contemporary philosophy. The book is completed by more detailed examinations of Aquinas's metaphysical system and his philosophy of mind.

HUME A. J. Ayer

A. J. Ayer begins his study of Hume's philosophy with a general account of Hume's life and works, and then discusses his philosophical aims and methods, his theories of perception and self-identity, his analysis of causation, and his treatment of morals, politics and religion. He argues that Hume's discovery of the basis of causality and his demolition of natural theology were his greatest philosophical achievements.

JESUS Humphrey Carpenter

Humphrey Carpenter writes about Jesus from the standpoint of a historian coming fresh to the subject without religious preconceptions. He examines the reliability of the Gospels, the originality of Jesus's teaching, and Jesus's view of himself. His highly readable book achieves a remarkable degree of objectivity about a subject which is deeply embedded in Western culture.

Past Masters

PASCAL Alban Krailsheimer

Alban Krailsheimer opens his study of Pascal's life and work with a description of Pascal's religious conversion, and then discusses his literary, mathematical and scientific achievements, which culminated in the acute analysis of human character and powerful reasoning of the *Pensées*. He argues that after his conversion Pascal put his previous work in a different perspective and saw his, and in general all human activity, in religious terms.

MARX Peter Singer

Peter Singer identifies the central vision that unifies Marx's thought, enabling us to grasp Marx's views as a whole. He views him as a philosopher primarily concerned with human freedom, rather than as an economist or social scientist. He explains alienation, historical materialism, the economic theory of *Capital*, and Marx's idea of communism, in plain English, and concludes with a balanced assessment of Marx's achievement.